THE PROPER CARE OF GERBILS
TW-106

The Proper Care of
GERBILS

Anmarie Barrie

636.9
B275
cop.3

Photo credits: Dr. Herbert R. Axelrod, Paul Bartley, Bob Bernhard, Isabelle Francais, Michael Gilroy, R. Hanson, D.G. Robinson, Jr., and Sally Anne Thompson.

Distributed in the UNITED STATES by T.F.H. Publications, Inc., One T.F.H. Plaza, Neptune City, NJ 07753; in CANADA to the Pet Trade by H & L Pet Supplies Inc., 27 Kingston Crescent, Kitchener, Ontario N2B 2T6; Rolf C. Hagen Ltd., 3225 Sartelon Street, Montreal 382 Quebec; in CANADA to the Book Trade by Macmillan of Canada (A Division of Canada Publishing Corporation), 164 Commander Boulevard, Agincourt, Ontario M1S 3C7; in ENGLAND by T.F.H. Publications, PO Box 15, Waterlooville PO7 6BQ; in AUSTRALIA AND THE SOUTH PACIFIC by T.F.H. (Australia) Pty. Ltd., Box 149, Brookvale 2100 N.S.W., Australia; in NEW ZEALAND by Ross Haines & Son, Ltd., 82 D Elizabeth Place, Panmure, Auckland, New Zealand; in the PHILIPPINES by Bio-Research, 5 ' Street, San Lorenzo Village, Makati, Rizal; in SOUTH AFRICA by Multipet Pty. .O. Box 35347, Northway, 4065, South Africa. Published by T.F.H. Publications, anufactured in the United States of America by T.F.H. Publications, Inc.

14.95
7/18/94
99

Contents

INTRODUCTION

There are many very common animals in pet stores and zoos about which little is known. One reason for this may be that even though these animals are common they have not been studied extensively. Such an example is the gerbil. Gerbils are a very attractive, popular pet with large dark eyes and a furry tail, but they have only recently been studied in any detail. In fact, their systematics was worked out during this century. They were first discovered in China and later introduced to the United States by Dr. Victor Schwentker for use in scientific research in 1954. Gerbils are still being used extensively in research and a fair amount of information about their carried diseases has been accumulated which is beneficial to humans. Gerbils are one group of rodents which in nature do not generally carry diseases that are harmful to humans. Other more basic research has also been done concerning their behavior and taxonomy. Gerbils have many interesting behaviors, which is one of the many reasons they are so popular as pets. They are also interesting from a taxonomic (systematic) point of view. They have a fairly definite preferred habitat and demonstrate many interesting adaptations to the areas in which they live. For this reason many scientists who study the relationships that similar species possess have devoted a considerable amount of time to the study of gerbil systematics.

Systematics

The gerbil is a member of the phylum Chordata, subphylum Vertebrata, class Mammalia, order Rodentia, suborder Myomorpha, family

Stocking a tank with gerbils should always be done with care.

Introducing Gerbils

The gerbil makes an ideal family pet. It is lively, but easy to keep and handle, inexpensive to buy and has a reasonably long lifespan. Gerbils can be kept satisfactorily by quite young children and provide an ideal introduction to the world of pets. Even the very smallest child will be fascinated by watching gerbils playing in their enclosure. Gerbils do not smell, unlike other members of the rodent family such as rats, and there are no significant diseases associated with them that could possibly be spread to people.

Facing page: Your pet shop can show you more books on gerbils—or, any other type of pet. You should be fully knowledgeable about your intended pet's needs before you purchase the animal.

HISTORY OF GERBILS

It's therefore not surprising that over the years, gerbils have achieved such a high level of international popularity as pets. In fact, the animal which is usually described simply as "the" gerbil is just one of over 80 different species found largely in dry areas of the world. This is the Mongolian gerbil (*Meriones unguiculatus*), a species native to the desert and semi-desert areas of Mongolia and northeastern China. Zoologists often know it better under the name of "clawed jird." These gerbils were first discovered as long ago as 1811, but it was not until 1935, when a Japanese zoologist visited the Amur River basin on the border of the U.S.S.R. and China that the species became known in captivity. He returned to Japan with 20 pairs of these rodents, which started to breed freely, and adapted well as laboratory subjects. In 1954, the West Foundation, New York, received 11 pairs from Japan for medical research, and soon colonies were established in other laboratories around the world.

Mongolian gerbils first became available to American pet owners about 1964. Then, slightly later, Europeans were also introduced to these delightful pets. A recent survey revealed that in Great Britain alone over a quarter of a million gerbils are being kept as pets.

Their worldwide population runs into many millions, and a variety of color forms have now been established successfully.

This has led to gerbils becoming popular as show animals, with the first major exhibition being staged in London by the National Mongolian Gerbil Society in 1971. Today, you can easily develop your interest in gerbils into establishing your own exhibition stud, competing at shows alongside other enthusiasts, and even training as a judge!

Gerbils have also been kept specially for working purposes because of their keen sense of smell. This idea originated from the Canadian government, which organized a scheme to train gerbils to detect drugs hidden in passengers' luggage at airports. The training scheme, which began in 1982, proved quite

Facing page: Gerbils are popular pets worldwide. Many gerbil fanciers have been bitten by the "show bug" and enjoy entering their pets in competition.

successful, but for the fact that the gerbils could only learn to recognize one odor each. As a result, luggage would have had to pass a whole battery of gerbils, each of which responded to a different scent.

Just when the role of the gerbil in drug detection appeared to be ending, however, the Canadian Federal Correction Service became involved. It arranged for the University of Toronto to train a small team of eight gerbils to monitor visitors who could be carrying drugs to prisoners. The team members were to press a warning button when they detected a drug.

The plan was to use them initially at a jail in the province of Ontario, but it ended up being scrapped again. On this occasion, the gerbils died prematurely from drinking poisoned water. Research into the use of gerbils in drug detection continued until 1984, at which time it was decided that monitoring the performance of the gerbils was too difficult.

GERBIL CHARACTERISTICS

The gerbil's keen sense of smell will enable him to find a favored item of food when you allow him out of his cage. In this way, you will soon develop an even closer bond with your new pet. Gerbils have short, almost hand-like paws which enable them to hold their food. In contrast, their hind limbs are much longer. This enables the gerbil to move quickly and to sit up on its haunches and feed,

Facing page: Gerbils can make good holiday gifts for children. They are hardy, intelligent, can get along well with children, and require a minimal amount of care and space. They are also inexpensive.

balancing with the aid of its long tail.

In its normal squatting posture, the gerbil's body appears hunched and rounded. The gerbil's relatively large eyes are set high on a broad head, so that the gerbil can see for a wide angle and which gives him an excellent field of vision. The small, rounded ears, which are very sensitive and can detect the slightest sound, are covered with soft hair.

The gerbil's keen senses, along with his camouflage coloration, help him to escape predators in the wild. His coat coloration enables him to blend into his natural environment. Golden brown hairs are admixed with black hairs. This color combination, which extends along the gerbils' tails, conceals them well. In contrast, their white belly fur, in contact with the warm ground, helps to reflect the daytime heat.

Gerbils are active both during the day and at night, resting for periods in their underground burrows throughout this time. They face many predators, ranging from foxes to polecats to birds of prey, including owls.

Coming from an arid part of the world, where water is in short supply, gerbils have evolved highly effective means of water conservation. Their kidneys produce very concentrated urine, ensuring that there is little accompanying loss of water. This is one of the reasons why gerbils are such clean animals, when compared with other pet rodents, and do not have an

Facing page: Originally, gerbils evolved to be camouflaged in their desert-like habitats; thus, their original coat is sand colored. Now they are available in many colors.

unpleasant odor associated with them.

Nevertheless, gerbils do have a scent gland on the lower part of their body, which may help members of a colony recognize each other. It is said to produce an odor somewhat reminiscent of the smell of burnt feathers! Gerbils also communicate by means of vibrations. They may drum the ground rapidly with their hind legs if threatened in any way, presumably as a warning to other gerbils which may be nearby. They also have a "peep"-sounding call, but are normally quiet animals.

As members of the extensive group of rodents, which comprise over 40 percent of all known mammalian species, gerbils have very effective teeth. The name "rodent" actually comes from the Latin word *rodere*, which means to gnaw. Their sharp front teeth, called incisors, are unusual because they continue growing throughout the gerbil's life. They are subjected to very heavy wear, gnawing through seeds, plants, roots and other food items.

Further back in the gerbil's mouth are the molar teeth. These grind the food into pieces which are sufficiently small enough to be swallowed. The toothless gap between incisors and molars, known as the diastema, allows the gerbil to close off its cheeks behind its front teeth. This in turn means that it can continue gnawing while the previous mouthful of food is still being ground up and swallowed.

Facing page: The Egyptian gerbil, *Gerbillus gerbillus*, is closely related to our pet gerbil from Mongolia, *Meriones unguiculatus*.

The modern gerbil gets larger and more colorful as it is inbred to suit the gerbil hobbyist.

Unlike some rodents, such as rats, however, gerbils are not seen as serious agricultural pests, even in areas where they are reasonably numerous. But you will need to bear in mind their destructive capabilities when choosing a suitable enclosure for them.

The other point you will need to consider in this context is that gerbils usually live in burrows. Here they can retreat during the day (when the sun is at is hottest), while condensation in the tunnels can provide valuable droplets of water. When concealed below ground, gerbils are also far less vulnerable to predators, of course, and have a relatively safe retreat where they can rear their young.

The temperature gradient here can be quite marked. Studies in the range of the Mongolian gerbil have

shown that there may be a temperature differential of 17°C (63°F) between the surface of the ground at midday, and a burrow located just 4 inches (10cm) below this point. But other creatures may also be attracted to the burrows, and some, notably snakes, will feed on gerbils.

Although little fieldwork has been carried out into the habits of many gerbil species in the wild, at least in the case of the Mongolian gerbil, it is clear that these rodents face so many hazards that their lifespan is very short. The majority of youngsters will not survive their first winter, and only a small proportion of the population are likely to live for a year.

In your home, however, your gerbil may live from three to five years. Several are on record as living for over eight years, such as

"Sahara," a female kept by a hobbyist in Michigan. It does appear that on average, females may live slightly longer than males, at least in domestic surroundings.

BUYING GERBILS

Most pet stores which have livestock will stock gerbils, but it may be a bit more difficult to locate species other than the Mongolian gerbil. Nevertheless, if you have one of the more rare species (or color varieties) in mind, ask your local pet store dealer, as he may be able to obtain your choice from a

This colorful male gerbil is protecting his mate while she sleeps. This is an unusual but not unnatural occurrence.

specialist supplier elsewhere in the country.

In the case of the Mongolian gerbil, do not be surprised if the pet store recommends purchasing more than one individual. This is not just "sales talk," since gerbils are very sociable creatures. They live in family communities in the wild, and will not thrive if they are kept on their own. If you do not wish to breed gerbils, it is easy to house two or three individuals of the same sex together.

Three-day-old gerbils. Within a few days their fur will begin to grow.

Try to obtain young gerbils; older animals may prove less social, and harder to tame, especially if they have not been used to being handled from an early age.

SEXING GERBILS

The gender of the gerbils is obviously important if you wish to prevent unwanted litters. Although both sexes appear quite similar at first glance, males tend to be slightly larger than females. You can confirm the gerbil's sex by examining the soft underbelly at the base of the tail.

You can hold a gerbil this way, but the animal can more easily slip from your grasp.

The ano-genital distance, which is simply the gap between the anus and the sex organs, will be longer in male gerbils. It measures about 10mm (.4 in), which is about double the length of the gap present in females. You will also be able to see the scrotum, formed by a covering of dark skin, which contains and protects the testes. The area here at the base of the tail is slightly enlarged, whereas it is rounded in the female.

HEALTHY GERBILS

Be sure that your prospective pets are healthy. Their eyes should be bright

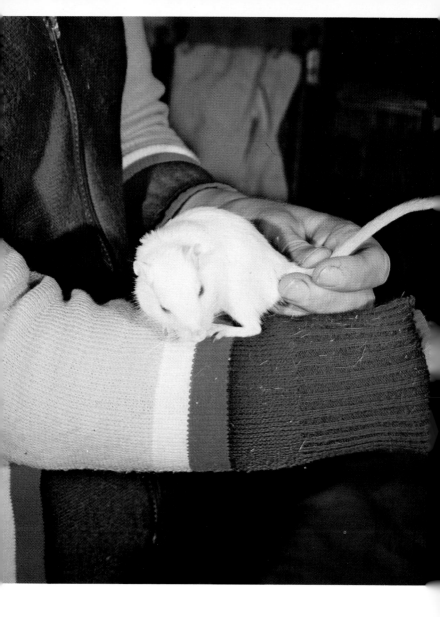

and their fur thick, soft, and shiny. The body itself ought to be plump and firm, ensuring that the gerbil does not appear emaciated in any way. Finally, watch the gerbils moving around their cage. A healthy gerbil is hardly ever still unless it is asleep. They are sensitive, inquisitive creatures, always exploring, nibbling, scrabbling, and reacting to every sound and movement in their vicinity. If you are offered a gerbil which does not behave in this way, do not be tempted to buy it, as it may be ill.

Finally, check the tip of the tail. This part of the gerbil's body can be injured very easily, and bleeds quite readily. The darker, bushy tip may act as a lure for predators in the wild, distracting them away from the gerbil's body. Should the gerbil lose the end of its tail, then it is not noticeably handicapped, although the tail is important for balancing.

TRANSPORTING GERBILS

A small cardboard box is not really suitable for taking your gerbils home. The holes provided for ventilation will allow the gerbils to gnaw at the cardboard. Once enlarged, these will then provide an easy exit point. Moving the gerbils in a cage will be safer, although alternatively, you can purchase special small rodent carriers for this purpose. They are usually made of plastic, and will have a ventilated hood and a sturdy built-in carrying-handle. If you are transporting gerbils regularly, such as back and forth to shows, then carriers

Facing page: The gerbil will feel more secure if it can get a firm grip on a solid surface.

of this type will be essential.

Some owners like to include a small cardboard box inside the actual carrier. By cutting off the flaps from one end, or making an entrance hole in the side, the gerbil can retreat within. A floor covering of some type is also to be recommended, so the gerbils are less likely to slide about on the base.

Although gerbils live in the warmer areas of the world, *never* leave them on the back seat (or elsewhere) in a vehicle with all windows shut. As with dogs and other animals, gerbils are likely to die from heat stroke, especially during the summer, as the temperature within the car will skyrocket within minutes.

A gerbil marking a small piece of wood with his scent imprint. The scent gland on his belly enables him to do this. He repeats the rub many times, scurrying back and forth repeatedly.

If the temperature is comfortable, your pet can be transported in a cage such as this. Naturally, a cage that offers more protection from the elements will be needed when the weather is unfavorable.

If your car has a trunk, also avoid placing the gerbils within it. Even though they will then be able to travel in the dark, there is the risk that exhaust gases will seep into this part of the vehicle. Carbon monoxide and other fumes could then spell rapid death for your new pets.

Finally, if you are travelling abroad and locate a gerbil of your choice in a pet store, remember that its transport across international boundaries is restricted. This is because, as with all other mammals, gerbils are potentially at risk from rabies, although the likelihood of them becoming infected is very, very slight. They would have to be bitten by a rabid animal, such as a dog, and survive this trauma if they were then to develop the disease.

There is no reason to be worried about this under normal circumstances, since gerbils are obviously kept apart from other animals. The vast majority of gerbils, in any event, are bred in captivity in the country concerned.

Shipping and quarantine costs preclude the purchase and transport of gerbils from foreign countries. If a hobbyist is seeking a particularly rare color variety, he should contact breeders within his own country. This also applies to some of the more unusual gerbil species.

There have also been fears expressed over the possible escape of gerbils in areas where they might

When you first get your gerbil home, give him time to become accustomed to you and his new surroundings. He probably only had other gerbils for company; now he has you.

establish themselves in the wild. In fact, some governing bodies have banned the ownership of gerbils as pets.

A small colony of Mongolian gerbils did become established for a period, however, on the Isle of Wight, off the south coast of England. The original animals were released after the filming of a natural history television program, and settled on waste ground and a nearby timber yard. But there appears to be no other occurrence of this type outside Great Britain.

This is a typical commercial gerbil cage available from many pet shops. Its only weakness is that the gerbil can escape when you lift the top off to clean it.

Housing Gerbils

There are several ways of keeping gerbils satisfactorily in the home, and you will need to decide as to which method suits you best. This also depends to some extent on the species which you are keeping, since gerbils do differ in terms of their requirements and also their destructive capabilities. The pallid gerbil, for example, digs much more actively than the Mongolian, and so is likely to scatter its bedding out of its quarters, if kept in a wire-mesh cage.

THE USE OF AQUARIA

In your local pet store, you will find a wide selection of suitable enclosures available to house gerbils, but probably the simplest option is to use an aquarium for this purpose. You can choose between glass and plastic tanks, although the glass ones tend to be more widely available, in a variety of shapes. You may even be able to acquire a triangular shaped tank, which will fit neatly in the corner of the room.

Remember that glass aquaria are relatively heavy. This may even be an advantage if you have young children in the home, since they will have difficulty in pulling an aquarium of this type on to the floor. In contrast, a plastic tank will be easy to dislodge off a surface.

Glass tanks are now almost universally made using a safe silicone sealant to hold the pieces together. This is fine for gerbils, provided that they do not gnaw at this material, because otherwise there is a possibility that they could weaken the bonding here. No such opportunity exists with plastic tanks, which are molded as a single unit. These are more easily scratched, however, and visibility through the sides can be spoiled as a result.

STOCKING DENSITY

The size of the enclosure depends on the number of gerbils which you intend to house together, bearing in mind their generally social natures. As a guide, it is usually recommended to allow about 36 sq. inches (230 sq. cms) for each gerbil.

Old aquaria are great for housing gerbils. The larger the aquarium the better. A top hood is recommended. Even though your gerbils cannot climb up glass and escape from the tank, other animals could get in!

For keeping a single gerbil, a small animal cage molded from clear plastic is ideal. There are many kinds of plastic cages. The cheapest easily crack (when you drop them) or scratch (when you clean them). The best are more resistant to cracking and scratching. A simple cover of wire mesh allows for the circulation of air and protects the gerbil from unwanted visitors.

This means that you can keep two together in an enclosure with minimum dimensions of 9 in. (22.5cm) long and 8 inches (20cm) wide, as an example.

If you do overcrowd them, then fighting is likely to occur, in spite of their normally friendly natures. Also, should you acquire more than one species, do not be tempted to mix them together, especially as there will be some variation in their size.

CAGE TYPES

You can house gerbils in the cages sold for hamsters, but remember that since hamsters are usually kept on their own, their cages tend to be relatively small. Choose from the largest cages available therefore, and check that the model you want has a reasonably deep base. This is important to allow the gerbils to burrow into the floor covering, and not scatter their bedding through the cage bars.

One of the best designs available does not have bars, but a clear plastic top with a

Gerbils love to play and chew. Even though they may delight in objects commonly found in the home, it is safest to provide play items specially designed for gerbils.

large, secure ventilation area and entrance point on the roof. The base is specially designed so that rodents cannot chew it easily, and for cleaning purposes it can be simply detached by means of clips.

A water bottle can be fitted in one of the corners of a cage of this type, whereas it is much harder to incorporate one securely in an aquarium. There is also no risk of the bottle becoming dislodged and possibly falling on a gerbil in the enclosure.

The base unit of these enclosures can alternatively be combined with a wire mesh surround, instead of the clear acrylic roof unit. This again clips on the sides in an identical fashion. But if you choose this option, you will also need not just a surround, but also a roof section, to fit on top of the surround. This will serve to

Pet shops have wonderful toys for gerbils. Pictured is part of a series of connected tubes through which the gerbil crawls, hides, sleeps, and plays.

Wooden toys or wooden cages are not recommended as a gerbil's urine soils the wood and causes odors. Gerbils easily gnaw wood and could escape from a wooden cage.

prevent the gerbils from escaping and will keep them safe from other pets, especially cats and dogs, which are likely to harm them.

These enclosures offer probably the best means of housing gerbils. They are secure, but easy to move, and can be cleaned thoroughly. At the same time, it is not difficult to move the gerbils in and out, and the relatively high sides help to prevent them from scattering their bedding to surrounding furniture.

Never be tempted to house gerbils in wooden cages of any type. As with all rodents, this type of accommodation is unsatisfactory. The gerbils will soon start using their sharp incisors on the wood, and may even manage to escape in a short period of time.

Wood is also absorbent,

unlike glass or plastic, so that their urine will soak into the floor and sides. Over a period of time, the cage will probably start to smell unpleasantly, and it will be hard to disguise this odor.

Although plastic is now widely used in cage design, you may occasionally see metal cages on offer. These used to be very popular. They look very attractive when new and certainly will not be chewed by the gerbils. But again, the gerbils's urine will lead to problems. Initially, it will attack the covering of paintwork and then will cause corrosion of the metal beneath.

Once this stage is reached, it is very difficult to maintain the appearance of the cage, and ultimately, holes with sharp, jagged edges will form on the cage floor. These are obviously

Gerbils are very curious animals. Even small shopping bags make for fun and games. Plastic-coated bags should not be used, as the plastic is indigestible for gerbils.

Gerbils can be compared to cats in terms of cleanliness. They are constantly grooming themselves. Healthy gerbils have immaculate coats that are kept clean by scratching and licking.

dangerous for the gerbils, and the cage will need to be replaced.

The lifespan of cages of this type depends to a large extent on the thickness of the covering of paintwork. It may be possible for you to add to the protection here by painting the base again using a non-toxic emulsion. Leave this to dry thoroughly, and repeat if necessary, before placing bedding on top. Generally, the more expensive cages of this type will have a better finish and should last longer than cheaper models.

Most commercially produced cages intended for gerbils and other small rodents are rectangular in shape, but you can also buy circular designs. The main drawback of these is that it can then be difficult to fit any toys inside, without occupying most of the floor space, unless the cage is very large. This can be overcome to some extent by the new style cages, which operate on two or even three levels, connected by tubes or ladders.

These may obviously resemble the gerbils' natural burrows, but you must be sure that they can move freely through the tubes, without fear of them becoming stuck at any point. The advantage of cages of this type is that you can expand them easily, which can be especially useful if you have an unexpected litter of young gerbils!

SETTING UP

Ideally, it is best to choose the gerbils' housing and set it up properly before buying the gerbils. If you have chosen to use a converted glass aquarium, it will be

Even though gerbils gnaw and urinate on wood, *temporary* wooden toys are useful. You can even make them yourself if you have a woodworking setup. Remember that toys made of wood should be discarded every few weeks or they will begin to give off an unpleasant odor.

particularly important to wash this out carefully, and leave it to dry, before setting it up for the gerbils. On occasion, sharp, tiny splinters of glass may remain in the aquarium, where they are almost invisible. Only by washing out the aquarium can you be virtually certain that you have removed them. Otherwise, they may harm your gerbils as they sniff around and explore their new quarters.

Similarly, if the cage appears dusty at all—having been on display in the pet store—then you should wash this as well. There are now several safe brands of disinfectant available for use with pet animals and stocked by pet stores. You simply add the recommended volume to the water when you wash the cage.

It is better to use pottery dishes than to use plastic dishes for your gerbil's feed. The pottery dishes are made for dogs and cats, but they serve very well for small animals like hamsters, gerbils, mice, rats, and guinea pigs.

A plastic feeding dish such as this can be extremely dangerous to gerbils. In the first case, the plastic itself may be poisonous to gerbils. In the second case, the gerbils could chew it up into small pieces that they could swallow—and it might impact their intestines.

Remember that clear acrylic cages can be easily clouded, however, by immersion in hot water, so use a tepid rather than boiling solution for this purpose. In addition, it is easy to scratch the plastic, so use a sponge rather than a cloth for wiping around the sides.

Finally, rinse the cage out thoroughly to remove any trace of the disinfectant solution, and allow it to drain. You can then wipe the sides dry with clean paper toweling, taking care to polish the clear acrylic sides to remove any traces of water droplets. These will otherwise spoil the appearance of the unit as they dry off. The same applies to the glass sides of an aquarium.

FLOOR COVERINGS

In the wild, of course, gerbils excavate burrows in the sandy desert soil, and they will show a similar tendency in your home, so that a reasonably deep floor covering is to be recommended. There are a range of suitable materials available for this purpose.

You could, of course, provide sand to a depth of several inches on the floor of the gerbils' enclosure. This enables you to create a fairly authentic environment, particularly in a large aquarium, and you can even add some large stones or pieces of rock.

Although it will probably not be possible to give the gerbils sufficient depth of sand in which to create real burrows, they will nevertheless enjoy scrabbling around here. But do be careful, however, to ensure that the sand does

This is the recommended type of exercise wheel for gerbils. The rungs and back of the wheel are one unit, thus preventing tail injury.

Gerbils use the exercise wheel in a manner different from hamsters. They climb into the wheel and tumble around as the wheel moves. This is especially exciting for young gerbils.

not become damp, either from the gerbils' urine, or by drips from their drinking bottle. This can otherwise cause their fur to become matted, spoiling their appearance, and may lead to them being chilled.

Damp sand is heavy, while of course, in an aquarium or similar container, it will tend to collapse readily when dry, handicapping the gerbils' tunneling attempts.

Cleaning out their quarters will need to be undertaken with particular care as well, since the grains of sand will easily scratch plastic, and even glass. The safest way to remove deposits is by washing or hosing out the enclosure.

Peat is another material favored by some gerbil keepers, and yet is less satisfactory than proprietary floor-coverings available from your local pet store. It is relatively sterile, but can turn moldy if it becomes damp and contaminated by organic matter, such as droppings or food. On a precautionary note, never be tempted to use garden soil, as this is full of potentially dangerous micro-organisms which could harm your gerbils.

Peat becomes very dusty as it dries out in the home, although it will prove absorbent. The fine particles may then lead your gerbils to sneeze repeatedly, by causing nasal irritation. Peat can also stain white fur, and this alone will make it unsuitable for use with show stock, especially white gerbils.

It is much better to rely on safe floor coverings sold by pet stores, marketed especially for gerbils and other small mammals. Sawdust can be used to create a snug cage lining,

Gerbils enjoy crawling into anything that resembles a tunnel. In their natural habitat they have tunnels connecting their sleeping quarters and their feed stores. They also use tunnels to escape from predators.

Like dogs, hamsters "mark" their territory. This is done by the use of a special scent gland on their underside.

and proves highly absorbent. But only coarse softwood sawdust is suitable for this purpose. Fine sawdust can cause irritation to the eyes and nose of the gerbils, as they burrow and explore their quarters.

Probably the best material for the floor of the gerbils' quarters is wood chips. Cedar is a popular wood for this purpose, with a pleasant fragrance which acts as a natural deterrent to insects. It is non-toxic, even for young gerbils. Packs of cedar chips are widely available from pet stores. You can buy them in pre-packed bags, or in compressed packs.

When opened, the compressed packs can be broken down simply by running the chips through your fingers and should prove the most economical means of purchasing this material. A greater volume can also be stored in a more limited space, which is helpful if you have a large collection of gerbils.

Never be tempted to purchase loose shavings or chips of unknown origins. This is because some timber is treated with chemicals which can prove poisonous for gerbils. If they nibble these chips, the outcome could be fatal, whereas you can be sure that those sold specially in pet stores are safe as cage litter.

BEDDING

Avoid using newspaper, because although it is cheap and absorbent, the printing ink may be harmful to the gerbils. They will almost certainly shred newspaper as well, making it into suitable bedding. Gerbils must be given safe material for this purpose, so they can make a snug nest. Pieces of cloth of any kind may contain harmful dyes.

Always avoid wool, be it in the form of knitting wool, cotton wool, or unspun fleece. It may appear to be an ideal bedding material, being warm, soft, and cozy, but as a result of chewing it, your gerbils are very likely to swallow some of the fine fibers. These will accumulate inside the stomach or intestine, creating a blockage.

If this is not removed rapidly, the outcome will be fatal. Should you suspect that your gerbil has unfortunately swallowed wool of some type, then seek veterinary advice without delay. The use of an effective laxative may free the obstruction, so your pet can recover from this trauma.

You should also not use wood wool as a bedding for gerbils. This material, often used to package delicate articles (especially in

Gerbils are curious, adventuresome little animals. They can literally spend hours exploring various nooks and crannies.

transit), is sometimes referred to as excelsior. It is unsuitable as bedding, proving neither warm nor absorbent. More significantly, the strands have very sharp edges, which can cut a gerbil's mouth or body. This applies especially to young gerbils in a nest, when their bodies are unprotected by fur.

As a final word of caution, avoid fiberglass, as an insulating or bedding material, where the gerbils could be exposed to it. This will prove very irritating to their skin, giving off sharp splinters and causing internal problems if swallowed.

Special safe bedding material for gerbils and other small animals can be obtained from your local pet store. If swallowed, this will not cause a blockage of any kind in the digestive tract. It may be in the form of natural fiber, or shredded paper bedding.

If paper is used, it will be of good grade, and will contain no dangerous chemicals. It must be relatively free from dust. Alternatively, you can buy paper strips of bedding, which your gerbils may find more appealing, as they can shred these lengths themselves.

Some breeders like to use hay as bedding for their gerbils, and this is also available in small quantities from pet stores. Only offer soft meadow-hay, since otherwise sharp ends of grasses and thistles are likely to result in injury. You should tease out the hay carefully before placing it within the gerbils' quarters, so as to remove any

Facing page: Sometimes a mother gerbil will separate her litter into two groups, giving each group equal attention. This litter of six has been split with three pups in each.

Gerbils love any kind of enclosure that affords them a sense of security and safety.

potentially dangerous pieces. It may be worthwhile shaking the hay outside in order to avoid exposing the gerbils to unnecessary dust. Be sure to keep the hay stored in a dry location, and if it appears at all moldy, it should be discarded.

Dry leaves are sometimes included as bedding, but although they may appear attractive for a short period of time, they will soon be destroyed by the gerbils. You must be certain, if you offer leaves in this way, that they are clean and not decaying. In addition, they should have originated from plants which are known to be non-poisonous.

Facing page: The shavings on the floor of this gerbil's home may be safe or poisonous, depending upon their source. Often, carpenter's shavings contain varnish, shellac, or paint and are detrimental to the health of gerbils.

This will depend on the area where you live, but avoid laburnum, lilac, and yew as examples. Leaves from fruit trees such as apple or pear should be quite safe, providing they have not been sprayed with chemicals. Avoid leaves with spikes (such as blackberry) and sharp pine needles, which could injure your pet.

OUTDOOR HOUSING

Gerbils come from a hot, dry climate and so need to be kept in warm quarters if they are housed outside. Depending where you live, it may be possible to construct an outdoor gerbil pen. Although you will not be able to have such close contact with your gerbils when they are kept in such surroundings, you will see them behaving more naturally.

Choose a sunny and sheltered spot for the pen. It is critical that the area will not flood, otherwise the gerbils are very likely to become badly chilled in a rainstorm, or even drown. It is often better to build a raised structure, above ground level as an added precaution, in case the water table is fairly high.

Cut away any turf, and level the site as necessary, digging out a base. You can then lay paving slabs over the floor area, which will ultimately serve to prevent the gerbils from tunneling out and escaping. Around the sides, you can build surrounding walls, using either bricks or blocks for this purpose. This seals the floor area and sides of the structure. The walls should be about 3 ft. (90cm) high.

Facing page: This inquisitive gerbil peeps out from the safe confines of his temporary hiding place.

You will then need to fill the base with a mixture of sand and earth, to a depth of 2 ft. (60cm). The actual mix will depend, to some extent, on the soil in your area. It is important that the substrate is not too fine, otherwise the gerbils will find it difficult to tunnel effectively. It may help initially to compact this base, and you can also add some rockery stones and weathered tree branches for landscaping on the surface. The gerbils will also enjoy climbing on these items.

Obviously the top of the pen needs to be covered, so as to protect the gerbils from cats and other likely predators. This can be simply achieved using wire mesh on a wooden framework. The timber should be one and one-half inches (3.75cm) square; it can be treated with a wood preservative to prolong its lifespan and enhance its appearance. You can either joint the lengths, which helps to prevent warping, or simply nail them together.

Use mesh which measures one-half inch (1.25cm) square to cover the framework. This is important, because otherwise there is a risk that wild

If wooden toys or pens are utilized, it is important that they have not been chemically treated. It will be necessary for you to investigate this very carefully as gerbils love to gnaw on wood.

rodents, especially mice, will be attracted to the food in the gerbils' enclosure. They may then introduce diseases to the gerbil colony, while rats might actually harm the gerbils themselves. By choosing a mesh which is fine, this should exclude even the youngest wild rodents. With secure foundations, they should also be unable to tunnel into the pen itself.

Aside from the mesh roof, part of the area should also

be covered with plastic sheeting, to provide some cover when it is raining. This will enable you to keep the gerbils' food dry and also gives some protection where they can retreat when necessary. The plastic can be easily fixed in place on the wooden framework, using the special supports which ensure that it should not crack when you drive the nails through it.

Holes for this purpose should be pre-drilled. As for wiring the frame, this is most easily carried out when the unit is lying flat on a level area of ground. Slope the plastic to ensure that rainwater runs away over the edge of the enclosure, rather than pouring onto the

At first glance, this gerbil seems to be captivated by the information on the computer screen. In reality, the contrasting lighting and movement on the screen have caught his eye.

If you are determined to let your gerbil out of his cage to play, it is essential that he is closely supervised.

floor inside. The simplest way of achieving this aim is to run an additional beam of timber beneath the plastic to raise it to a higher level over the run, compared with the perimeter of the enclosure.

Finally, you will need to secure the roof section to the sides of the structure. This is important, because if it can be dislodged, the gerbils will be at risk from predators. Some animals, such as foxes, are very adept at finding weaknesses in livestock enclosures, in order to prey on the occupants. You will need to open the roof quite regularly, and so easy access to the interior is equally important.

Start by placing two hinges on the frame on one side, and fix these also to the outer face of the corresponding wall. You can use masonry nails for this purpose, although it will help if you have already started to make the necessary holes. On the opposite side of the structure, you can either use a hasp and padlock, preferably of the combination type so that you will not need to worry about a key, or a straightforward sliding bolt, which simply drops down, securing the roof section in place.

HOUSING A LARGE COLLECTION

If you build up a large collection of gerbils, it may not be possible to accommodate them indoors, and yet outside housing as described above also could be impractical. This applies especially if you are trying to develop a strain of a particular color, for exhibition purposes. You will then need to be able to keep a check on pairings, rather than simply setting up a large colony of gerbils and allowing them to mate at random.

You may then decide to convert an outbuilding to house your collection of gerbils. A shed in the backyard is suitable for this purpose, provided that it is built on a solid concrete base, so that other rodents will find it difficult to gain access to the interior. As a further precaution, store seed and other foodstuffs in metal bins.

Most sheds tend to be rather cold in the winter in

Facing page: Gerbils can be profitable for the hobbyist breeder if he specializes in rare color varieties.

temperate climates. You may need to install a heater. Probably the most suitable is the tubular convector type. The heating element is contained within a sealed metal tube. It is therefore not affected by dust in the environment, unlike fan-type heaters, and presents no direct hazard to any gerbils which might escape in the shed.

With all heating systems that incorporate electrical cord, you should take the precaution of "gerbil-proofing" the cord: a stray gerbil could try to gnaw through it with catastrophic consequences. You can either run the cord behind a plastic PVC conduit or cover it with a flexible metal casing.

It is recommended that you insulate the interior of the shed, because otherwise, your heating costs are likely to be substantially increased. Cover the walls and roof with a standard insulation quilt, taking care to follow the recommended precautions when working

Mazes are an excellent means of keeping your pet gerbil mentally stimulated and well exercised. Mazes that are designed for mice and rats can also be used for gerbils. Your local pet shop can offer you a wide array of toys and other entertainment devices suitable for gerbils.

with this material. You can then line the inside of the shed with hardboard or a similar material, concealing the insulation behind this lining. If you decide to paint these sheets, then choose a pale color which will brighten the interior of the shed.

Other areas of heat loss from the building will include the door and windows. Check that the door closes snugly therefore, with no obvious gaps visible from the outside. Apart from allowing heat to escape, these gaps also produce drafts, which can prove harmful to gerbils. It may be possible to install draft excluders, or alternatively, fit a bolt near the bottom of the door, on the outside, which will help to hold it properly closed.

The windows in the shed should open when necessary, helping to provide ventilation. During the colder part of the year, however, you may want to cover the inside of the glass

Even though gerbils are accustomed to living in close quarters, a cage that is this crowded is not good for its occupant. Your pet needs room to move about.

with special plastic sheeting.

You might also need a light in the shed, especially at the time of year when daylight hours are of shorter duration. Unless you are certain of the correct procedure, do not attempt to run electrical cable from your domestic supply to the shed. Seek the help of a qualified electrician. For the sake of safety, there are various regulations in force which cover such work.

Finally, in terms of electrical equipment, it is advisable to include a

Gerbils are remarkable acrobatic artists. Notice how this little fellow uses his claws for the purpose of balancing.

thermostat in the circuitry. This will serve to switch the heater on automatically once the temperature in the shed falls to a pre-set figure and will also turn it off once an upper level is reached. This means that there is no need to worry about having to switch the heater on in a sudden cold spell and also provides an economical control, by restricting the output of heat when it is not required. As a guide, the thermostat should be set to operate somewhere within the range of 40-50°F, depending partly on whether or not the gerbils are breeding.

OUTFITTING THE INTERIOR

Tubular heaters are usually positioned close to the floor, so that the air warmed as a result of their operation then rises through the building. Floor-mounting may be possible, but it is more usual to attach them by brackets to the side of the structure. The brackets can be screwed onto the vertical supports of the shed.

The thermostat will have to be attached in a similar fashion, but obviously, you must locate this at a point well away from the heaters. Otherwise, it will tend to switch off the heater too soon, before the whole area is properly warmed.

The light switch should be located at a convenient height close to the door, and the lighting cable itself should be run up to the roof, with the unit itself being fixed securely to a beam. You can use either an ordinary incandescent bulb or a fluorescent light. Alternatively, you may wish to choose one of the types of full-spectrum fluorescent tubes now available. You

A gerbil may enjoy being put into a box where the cover or lid is not affixed, but this is not a good idea. Imagine the disaster if the gerbil couldn't get out, and there is not enough air for it to live very long!

The light your gerbil receives is important to its health. The ultraviolet segment of sunlight stimulates the production of vitamin D, which is necessary for mammalian life.

should be able to obtain these quite easily from aquatic stores especially, as they are popular for reptiles and fish.

Full-spectrum fluorescent tubes are similar in their spectral range to that of sunlight. In turn, the ultra-violet component of sunlight stimulates the manufacture of Vitamin D on mammalian skin. This vitamin is vital in coordinating calcium and phosphorus levels in the body. (A deficiency of this vitamin can result in a disease known as rickets.)

Although it is possible to add Vitamin D to a gerbil's diet, these full-spectrum fluorescent tubes may nevertheless act as a tonic for these rodents, which would normally be exposed to quite high levels of sunlight in their natural environment. Therefore, if you do include lighting, this type is well worth considering, using no more electricity than and having an equivalent lifespan to a normal bulb or tube of the same wattage.

Since you will be housing a number of pairs of gerbils within the shed, you will require some sort of shelving to make the best available use of the space. Again, as with a heater, you must attach the shelving to the vertical supports in the shed, unless it is to be free-standing.

Alternatively, you can place horizontal struts behind the lining, if present, and this provides a more versatile means of attachment. Bear in mind that while one cage may not be very heavy on its own, ten in a row will certainly need adequate support.

The shelving can be simply constructed of metal brackets and suitable

Gerbils are scavengers and will eat anything they ascertain is tasty. It is up to you, their keeper, to ensure that their diet is wholesome and balanced.

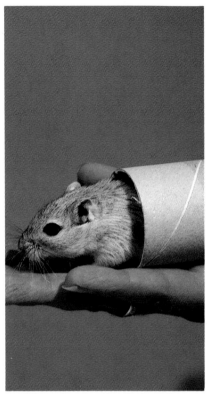

When planning the design of your pet gerbil's housing, be sure to allot space for toys and other cage accessories.

lengths of timber. Start by fixing the brackets in place, and then varnish the timber outside, and leave it to dry thoroughly. The varnish will effectively seal the pores in the wood, making it easier to keep clean. But be certain not to use treated timber of this type in a location where gerbils may gnaw at it, since it could prove harmful to them.

As an alternative to timber, you may prefer to consider industrial steel shelving. This item is stocked by a variety of different types of stores. It offers a fairly flexible system, complete with adjustable shelves, which means that you can save on floor space. Food bins can be kept on the lower levels, with the cages stacked above.

When planning the design of shelving, however, you must also consider the cages themselves. It is important that you can easily service these and also see their occupants without difficulty. Cages designed with an access door on the top of the unit are likely to require more space than those which open at the front.

Steel shelving is relatively expensive, but it should prove very durable. You must ensure that the floor on which it is to be stood is level, however, because this will directly influence its stability. It is usually supplied in kit form, and you can either purchase complete units or individual components to make up your own dimensions.

The shelving is actually very easy to assemble with a wrench, being held together by nuts and bolts. If you suspect that the floor is slightly uneven, or simply for extra stability, you can

While gerbils do not require spacious housing, it is very helpful to have flat rocks on different levels so that they can exercise as they climb from one level to the next.

Do *not* locate a gerbil cage in a sunny area unless there are places where the animals can hide from the sun's rays should they become overheated.

usually also screw the framework at a convenient point to one of the supporting bars in the shed.

Although gerbils are found in desert areas, where the temperature rises considerably during the day, they do not like being subjected to direct sunlight. Under these conditions, they will suffer and succumb to heat stroke.

It is therefore advisable, when planning the layout of a shed, to avoid positioning their cages in a position directly in front of a window. This applies especially if you are housing them in a glass aquarium, since the glass will magnify the warming effect of the sun's rays, and is likely to raise the temperature rapidly to a fatal level. During the winter months in temperate climates, however, the situation is somewhat reversed. A location directly in front of the window is then likely to be one of the coldest spots in the shed, and so it is not really suitable for cages at this time of the year either. In any event, it will be useful to have a bench or table available, to assist when you are cleaning out gerbils' quarters or assessing their show potential. This is best located in front of the window, so that you can see the gerbils as much as possible in natural light, which reveals their true coloration. The space here can then be wisely utilized.

You can make a suitable bench quite easily, using a plywood sheet mounted on legs. Another simple but very useful piece of equipment will be a plastic cat-litter tray, available from pet stores, which fits snugly within thin plywood surrounds about 1 foot

Gerbils need fresh air that is well ventilated. This is especially true if they are kept in an aquarium-like environment that does not have circulating air.

(30cm) tall. This makes straightforward temporary accommodation for gerbils while you clean out their quarters, with little risk of them escaping. The plastic litter tray can also be wiped over easily, preventing any spread of infection by this route.

VENTILATION

In the summer months, it may be advisable to leave the shed door open for periods during the day, to reduce the internal temperature. This tends to be more effective than simply opening a window, while opening the two together establishes a current of air. But in either case, you will need to protect the gerbils from the unwanted attentions of cats and other predatory animals in the vicinity.

An inner door made of a wooden framework covered

Gerbils love to gnaw and chew on virtually anything within their reach. Thus, a wood cage is not advisable for housing gerbils, as the occupants will surely damage it.

If you are going to provide your gerbil with toys that he can tunnel through, make sure the passageways are large enough for him to easily maneuver.

with one-half inch (1.25cm) square mesh will be ideal for this purpose. It must be hung with brackets in such a way that you can close this inner door without affecting the opening or closing of the outer door.

In terms of fixtures, obtain a hook and clasp, as well as a straight post. These items will enable you to hold the outer door firmly open, with the hook, attached to the door, fixing into the clasp positioned on the post.

This is important, because otherwise a sudden gust of wind can blow the outer door closed, so that it slams against the framework of the shed. Apart from damaging the structure, the resulting noise will scare the gerbils, especially as they have very sensitive hearing.

On the inner door, fix two sliding bolts at the top and bottom, rather than relying on just one in the middle. Especially if the framework is warped in any way, a cat may otherwise have little difficulty in pushing its way thru the gap between the frame and inner door. Even if it is then not able to harm the gerbils, its presence will upset them, especially if it walks over their cages.

It is possible to incorporate a degree of automatic ventilation into the design of the shed. This can be particularly valuable if you are not at home for most of the day. You will need to replace the conventional shed windows, however, with those which operate automatically. Irrespective of whether or not you choose automatic windows, the windows in question will need to be protected with wire mesh if they are to be used for ventilation purposes. In the case of a single window which opens off an arm, then you will probably be

When holding a gerbil, a secure grip is required, but do not exert undue pressure on the animal.

Compared to other pets, the housing requirements of gerbils are notably minimal.

able to tack the mesh directly around the window frame. Simply cut a small hole sufficient to reach the end of the arm and keep the window open.

The situation will be more difficult, however, if you need to lift the windows out. Then you will have to make a suitable frame covered with mesh, so the unit itself is removable. Obviously, it will also have to be capable of being fixed firmly in place, otherwise the frame could be dislodged by the wind when the window was removed. But since you will want to avoid having to keep re-screwing the frame into place, bolts again provide the simplest means of removing it as necessary.

FINISHING TOUCHES

If the shed comes complete with a wooden floor, you may decide to add a covering of linoleum on top. This will then make

it much easier to keep the floor clean, as there will be no cracks where dirt could accumulate. You can even mop and disinfect the floor at regular intervals to keep the gerbils' surroundings spotless.

Finally, depending on where you live, it may be advisable to fit a door- and possibly a window-lock as well, to deter a break-in by vandals. Having to undo the lock when you enter the shed every time may be an inconvenience, but it will be nothing compared to the heartbreak you will experience if your collection of gerbils is vandalized. Rather than choose a lock which needs a key, you can instead opt for a suitably robust combination lock, which should prove less of a nuisance to open on a regular basis.

Above: This gerbil has been poorly fed on a high carbohydrate diet (too much corn!). It is fat and unhealthy looking. **Facing page:** This gerbil is being offered a balanced diet with lots of different foodstuffs.

Feeding Gerbils

Few animals are as easy to feed as gerbils. They are not expensive to look after, and far less wasteful than hamsters because they do not generally store food in their bedding. In the wild, gerbils consume a variety of seeds, roots and plant material, and some also eat insects on occasion.

Every gerbil-keeper has a different way of feeding his pets, and this will depend to some extent on the numbers which you have in your collection. It's much easier to provide a varied diet if you own just two or three gerbils rather than a hundred or more. But in all cases, it will be essential to provide a balanced diet so that your stock remains in peak condition. A poorly-nourished gerbil will neither breed successfully nor win show prizes.

The simplest way to feed a few pet gerbils is to try a

commercially-packaged mix from your local pet store. There are various brands available, although their ingredients tend to be similar. They contain a

make your own mixture.

Store this carefully, especially if you have a bulk supply, so that it will not deteriorate or attract other rodents, notably rats and

In their natural desert-like environment, gerbils spend most of their daytime hours in their burrows, where it is relatively cool.

mixture of seeds which are specially blended for gerbils.

Should you own a large number of gerbils, it is likely to be cheaper to buy the individual seeds in bulk, and blend these together to

mice. This is especially likely in outdoor surroundings, such as in a garden shed. Avoid using sacks, since these will be easily destroyed by rodents. If they contaminate the food with their urine and

Fresh fruit can upset the digestive system of a gerbil and should be offered in very small quantities. Fresh fruit should be considered a treat food, not a mainstay of the diet. This is a cinnamon gerbil.

droppings, it can then represent a threat to your health, as well as that of your pets.

In addition, seed is more likely to become damp in paper sacks. You may spill water over the sack, or the sack) inside it. Here it will be out of reach of rodents and remains free from dampness. Use all the seed from one packet before starting another. This ensures that the gerbils' food is as fresh as possible,

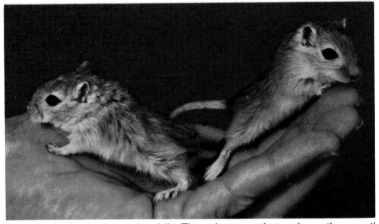

An inquisitive pair of agouti gerbils. The color tones that make up the agouti coloration are clearly visible.

roof may develop a leak, and wet seed will soon turn moldy.

It is best to invest in a metal bin with a lid and simply store the food (in a since the nutritional value of the seeds does not improve with age.

In addition, there is then less risk of fodder mites becoming established in the seed and transferred to the gerbils' quarters. It is unclear as to whether these tiny mites cause any direct harm, but certainly they may cause skin irritation, should they be transferred from the seed to the gerbil's them. Examine a seed sample in your hand. It should be clean, free from dust, and have no noticeable odor.

If you do suspect mites are present, you may be able to see them on closer

There are many color shades, and many of them are related to browns. Some gerbil breeders name the color varieties by the same color names used for minks.

body as the gerbil feeds.

The mites are hard to spot; you are more likely to detect their presence by the unusually sweet and rather sickly smell associated with examination, especially with a magnifying glass. They are just visible to the naked eye and move through the seed debris; as a result, they are often concentrated at the bottom of a bag.

It is probably safest to discard contaminated seed and then wash out the storage bin. Otherwise, with permanent access to a food supply, the mites will thrive and grow rapidly in numbers. Special preparations to kill mites are available from pet stores. Carefully follow the directions on the package.

PROVIDING A BALANCED DIET

The vital components of any healthy diet are carbohydrates, fats, proteins, vitamins, and minerals, as well as water. Carbohydrates, which are the major ingredient of cereals (grains), are important to meet the body's activity demands, as an energy source. Excess carbohydrate in the diet can be converted to fat.

Oil seeds, such as sunflower, are a valuable source of vegetable fats, and provide a concentrated source of energy, helping to maintain body temperature, for example, during cold weather. Fat is also important to protect body organs such as the kidneys from trauma, but excessive fat is harmful, resulting in obesity and circulatory problems.

Proteins are made from components called amino-acids. An adequate level of dietary protein is especially important both for breeding gerbils and youngsters. Otherwise, the reproductive rate is likely to be poor and the young gerbils will not thrive. There is even the possibility of an increased risk of cannibalism by the

Facing page: Gerbils use their forepaws to eat. They can open a sunflower seed and eat it in a few second's time...just as fast as squirrels can.

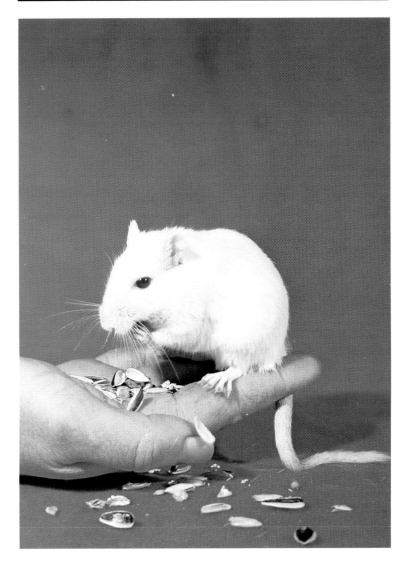

adults in the rarer species, if the protein level of their diet is too low.

Vitamins fulfill a wide range of functions in the body. Members of the Vitamin B group, for example, are involved in metabolic reactions, forming a vital part of the process of the breakdown of foodstuffs in the body. Vitamin D, in contrast, is needed to regulate body stores of calcium and so is essential for healthy bone structure. Both vitamins A and C help the body to resist infections, while Vitamin K plays a vital role in the blood clotting process. Vitamin E may be important for fertility, but it is also involved with metabolic processes and muscle function.

Some foods are deficient in certain vitamins. Cereals, for example, contain low levels of Vitamin A. While

Gerbils are almost always eating…and almost always shedding their waste. Often they contaminate their own feed and scatter it about their cage bottom.

some vitamins, such as C and K, can be made in the body, others must be present in the diet if a deficiency is not to occur. Providing a good varied selection of foods will help to ensure that your gerbils do not suffer from any shortage of vitamins.

Similarly, minerals have many roles to play in the body. Calcium, as one example, is well known to be an essential ingredient of bone. But it is also necessary for muscle contraction, as are sodium and potassium.

Trace elements are basically needed in smaller amounts than minerals, but are equally vital in ensuring that the body remains healthy.

Iodine, for example, is needed by the thyroid glands in the neck, for the manufacture of thyroid hormones, which in turn affect organs around the body. Selenium, in conjunction with Vitamin E, is required in small amounts for healthy muscles.

FOOD MIXES

If you decide to prepare your own food for the gerbils, then the following mix will provide a good basis to meet your pets' nutritional requirements. Wheat and oats or barley, in equal quantities, should form the basis of the diet, accounting for about fifty percent of the mix.

In addition to these cereals, you can provide a small amount of maize (fifteen percent). This is a relatively hard seed, and chewing it should also help to keep the gerbils' teeth from becoming overgrown. Maize is a valuable source of carbohydrate and may provide some Vitamin A as well.

Wheat, of course, is known for its Vitamin E content, which is sometimes marketed under the name of "wheat germ oil." Oats have a high carbohydrate content, also containing lesser amounts of protein and fat like the other cereals. It may be better to choose groats, which are simply oats with the course outer husk removed, or crushed oats, rather than whole oats.

Facing page: Gerbils enjoy fresh leafy vegetables of many varieties. This lovely black gerbil is feasting on raw lettuce.

Gerbils can be taught to eat when you want to feed them. They will stand up and "beg" for food when you come near their cage.

These will be easier for gerbils to eat, and there is less wastage, as well as the bonus that the potentially sharp oat husks cannot injure your pet.

Pelleted food, produced for many types of rodents, has become more widely-available during recent years. It is a valuable supplement to the diet.

But be certain not to use any medicated pelleted foods, for example, those containing drugs against coccidosis, unless recommended by your veterinarian. In some countries, such as Great Britain, they are only available on prescription in any event.

If you find it difficult to obtain rodent pellets, then as an alternative, you can use rabbit pellets, which are widely available from virtually all pet stores. They are round or oval in shape, and made from items such as grass meal and chaff, mixed with vitamins and minerals, which make a particularly valuable addition to the diet.

Not all gerbils will eat pellets readily, but those which do so will receive the benefit. It is a good idea to introduce pellets to young gerbils, as they are often more ready to eat unfamiliar items than adults, whose feeding patterns are well-established.

The proportion of fat in the diet of gerbils needs to be restricted, because otherwise your pet will become obese, and its lifespan is likely to be shortened as a result. This is especially significant in the case of gerbils living indoors in the home, where they will be expending little energy on keeping warm.

Although gerbils often prefer sunflower seeds to

To keep your gerbil healthy and happy, you must provide it with a well-balanced diet.

Black-and-white-striped sunflower seeds are a common food for gerbils and other small mammals. They are a great food, but white sunflower seeds are even better as they are higher in protein.

other foods, you should restrict the quantity in the mix to less than ten percent of the total for this reason. As an oil seed, sunflower is a rich source of fat, although it also contains significant amounts of protein. There are various forms of sunflower seed available.

The black and white striped variety is most often used as small mammal food, but if you can obtain white sunflower seed, this will be better, especially for breeding and young gerbils. It has a higher protein content than the striped form, although it may also be slightly more expensive, because the yield from a field tends to be lower.

You can also add a few peanuts to the seed mix. Gerbils like to nibble peanuts, also known as groundnuts, because although the flowers are fertilized in the air, the resulting seed pods then develop on the stems below ground. You can offer either the dried pods, or just the nuts within. Some gerbils will even feed on these nuts from your hand, although it is better to offer the whole pod at first, because there is then less risk of your pet biting your finger accidentally.

Only choose top quality peanuts and be particularly sure to keep them dry. Moldy peanuts are potentially very dangerous, as they may contain powerful poisons called aflatoxins, which damage the liver, frequently with fatal results. Also, never be tempted to offer gerbils salted nuts of any kind, as this could be equally harmful to your pets' health.

Note the size of this albino gerbil. In general—with most species— albino animals are smaller than those that are normally colored.

FRESH FOODS

Try to provide some fresh food for the gerbils on

Close-up view of a healthy, active gerbil. If you have any doubts about the suitability of your pet's diet, check with your pet shop dealer.

a regular basis. Greenfood is a valuable source of vitamins, such as Vitamin A, and helps to compensate for deficiencies present in seed. It also contains many of the minerals vital for healthy body functions, including zinc, copper, iron, calcium, phosphorus, and sodium.

Although relatively low in terms of carbohydrate, fat, and protein, greenfood consists of a large amount of water, often as much as eighty percent. In the arid areas where they live in the wild, gerbils will often seek out plants which provide them with essential water.

For the pet gerbil, you can offer two different groups of greenfood. Firstly, there are those which are cultivated as vegetables for human consumption. These you can either purchase, or grow yourself, even on a window ledge if necessary. Parsley is easily cultivated in this way, while you can generally buy lettuce, cabbage, cauliflower, chicory, brussel sprouts, and spinach throughout the year.

If you decide to grow spinach, choose seeds of a strain which is low in oscalic acid. This particular chemical can otherwise interfere with the absorption of calcium from the gut, and could prove harmful, especially for young gerbils. Root vegetables, such as carrots, can also be given.There are strains which you can grow easily from seed which have raised levels of Vitamin A, and these are especially valuable for gerbils.

Other root vegetables, such as turnips and swedes, are also useful, giving the gerbils an opportunity to gnaw, but do not feed raw potatoes, as these could be harmful. Scrub and rinse such vegetables, and then

The green grass contains water and is especially attractive to gerbils as a food. The straw, which is essentially dried grass, has no attraction unless the gerbil is starving.

You cannot fulfill your gerbil's nutritional requirements by feeding him just one type of food. For example, sunflower seeds are a good source of protein, but they have a considerable fat content. A diet of sunflower seeds only can result in an overweight gerbil.

This gerbil's coat is smooth and glossy—the result of proper dietary care.

cut them into small sections which the gerbils can eat easily. Do not provide large amounts, but offer a small quantity on a regular basis so as not to upset your pet's digestive system.

A number of wild plants can also be collected for gerbils, but you must choose areas where dangerous chemicals will not have been used. Avoid roadside verges therefore, since not only may these have been sprayed with herbicides, but the vegetation here usually contains abnormally high levels of lead. This chemical is likely to build up in your gerbils' bodies over a period of time, with potentially harmful consequences.

It may be better to seek out such plants among flower beds in your backyard. Weeds like dandelion, shepherd's purse, groundsel, chickweed, and plantain can

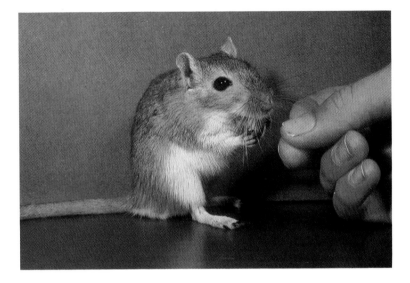

Facing page: A pregnant gerbil nibbling on a bit of lettuce. Providing a pregnant gerbil with a nutritious diet can help to ensure that she will have healthy offspring (barring genetic defects). **Above:** It is not at all difficult to teach your pet to take food from your hand.

all prove valuable additions to the gerbils' diet. Dandelion, as one example, is an important source of various vitamins, notably A, B and C, and will also help to cure constipation and overcome some liver ailments.

If you want a supply of such plants through the colder months of the year, then it is often possible to grow them in containers

indoors. Although some specialist seed merchants offer these wild plants on their lists, you can alternatively collect seed yourself during the summer, or propagate them from existing plants.

In order to grow dandelions, for example, all you really need is a piece of root. Set this in a reasonably large pot of soil, about one-half inch (1.25cm) below the surface, water it, and place the pot inside a plastic bag. Within a week or so, depending on the

Above: In the small-pet world, gerbils are quite easy to feed. This ivory female is keeping a watchful eye on her companion. **Facing page:** This lovely white gerbil represents only one of the many color varieties of gerbils from which you can choose.

temperature, you will see the green shoots appearing on the surface.

Remove the pot from the plastic bag at this stage, so that the young shoots do not become moldy, and keep it moist. Soon you will have a large plant, from which you

When feeding your gerbil greenfood, be sure to wash it first. You don't want to risk your pet's health by letting him ingest any food items that have been chemically treated.

can pick leaves at regular intervals.

If you set up several such cultures in succession, you will be guaranteed an almost constant supply of fresh greenfood throughout the year. Under these circumstances, there is really no need to wash it before feeding it to your pets. But greenfood from outdoors should always be washed, in case it has been fouled by other animals, or could be contaminated with manure or fertilizers.

Always be certain to collect only fresh leaves, avoiding any which are showing signs of fungus or other disease. For example, it is probably best not to use dandelions which are showing signs of mildew (a fungal infection) on their leaves. This is evident as a series of white spots over the surface.

In addition, although

much that is green can be used safely, some plants should always be avoided because they will be poisonous for small mammals. This applies particularly to plants grown from bulbs, such as tulips, daffodils, crocuses, bluebells, and hyacinths. You should also avoid belladonna (deadly nightshade), poppies, bindweed, rhubarb, and lobelia.

Gerbils often prefer young, tender leaves and stems to coarser vegetation, which tends to be of less nutritional value, although it is high in fiber. Avoid using frosted greenfood as well, because this could well upset your pets' digestive system.

Gerbils have various preferences when it comes to food. Many of them enjoy grain-type foodstuffs.

OTHER ITEMS

As occasional treats, there are a number of other items which you can offer to

In general, adult gerbils are attentive, protective parents.

your gerbils. Wholemeal bread, baked hard in the oven and allowed to cool, is especially useful because it will encourage your pets to use their teeth and will help prevent the teeth from becoming overgrown.

You can also offer plain sweet biscuits, but avoid any with a sweet filling or chocolate. Do not offer a whole biscuit; instead, feed a small piece.

You can supplement their food mix with other seeds, such as millet sprays, which are more usually sold by pet stores as bird food. A budgerigar feed mix can also be added to their normal food. In addition, you will find a range of special treats available at your pet store.

These not only provide valuable variety to the gerbils' diet, but also encourage them to exercise and wear down their teeth.

Honey sticks are among the most popular, and are usually mounted on a wooden support, around which a blend of seeds, nuts and even dried vegetables are set in a honey base, frequently supplemented with essential minerals.

Some gerbils also enjoy a little fruit on occasion. You can provide small pieces of sweet apple, or even a few grapes, although be certain to wash them thoroughly first. Remove any uneaten fruit at the end of the day, before it can start to turn moldy.

Although Mongolian gerbils are essentially vegetarian, a few breeders have found that some will eat invertebrates, notably mealworms, which are the larval form of the meal

Facing page: Although some gerbils are found in low-lying grasslands, their most typical habitat is that of the desert.

A curious pair of gerbils exploring their desert-like habitat.

beetle (*Tenebrio molitor*). These are widely sold by pet stores, often as bird food, and can be kept easily in a plastic container of chicken meal, or plain bran although this is less nutritious for them.

A slice of apple on the surface should provide sufficient moisture for the mealworms. It is important to keep them in a cool spot to slow their development, because otherwise they will change into white, inert pupae before emerging as adult beetles.

If you keep some of the more unusual species of gerbil, you may find that

Below: A normal Mongolian gerbil. Unlike their brothers in the wild, domesticated gerbils have periods of activity in both daytime and nighttime. **Facing page:** A good diet will provide the "fuel" for your gerbil, which, by nature, is a very active animal.

they are keener on such foods than the Mongolian. Certainly, should you find that they cannibalize their own offspring, then offer mealworms. It could be that a shortage of animal protein in the diet is the cause of this abnormal behavior, assuming the breeding gerbils were not being disturbed excessively.

Only offer two or three mealworms at a time; otherwise, they could escape from the cage, into the home. Although they will not cause any damage, their presence here is obviously not to be recommended.

FEEDING ROUTINE

Gerbils in any event have very small appetites. As a rough guide, each will eat about the equivalent of one tablespoon, or 0.3oz (8g) of food daily. They should always have a pot of food available, although individual feeding patterns

An empty tissue box makes the perfect playhouse for this gerbil. Gerbils have a wonderful ability to amuse themselves—and their owners!

Letting your gerbil freely roam around in high places—in this case, a bed—can be disastrous. Your pet could fall off and injure itself.

do vary somewhat. Their natural curiosity means that they will usually venture to the food container after you have refilled it and will eat immediately. They then feed throughout the day at intervals.

Each animal is likely to have its own favorites and dislikes in terms of food. Watch your gerbils carefully

Two dove gerbils and a cinnamon gerbil. The difference in coloration is readily apparent.

at feeding time, and be prepared to experiment with extra items. You will soon discover their individual preferences.

If your cage does not come equipped with a self-attached food bowl, then it is best to choose a small ceramic pot. The gerbils will be unable to tip this over, and it will be easy to wash out when necessary. Plastic containers should be avoided because they can be easily destroyed by the gerbils' sharp teeth.

Stainless steel pots are also relatively light, and can be emptied easily, with their contents being scattered around the floor of the cage.

Be sure to select a reasonably small container;

Facing page and above: Gerbils, like mice and rats, will eagerly explore a maze. You might want to place a food treat in the maze as a reward.

otherwise you will not be able to easily lift it through the cage door. This then complicates the task of feeding and increases the risk of the gerbils escaping into the room.

WATER

The simplest means of providing water is to use a

special drinking bottle, available from most pet stores. You simply fill the glass or plastic container with water, and seal it with the special spout at the base. Finally, turn the drinker so that you can hook it into position through the bars of the cage. The spout should be directed just above floor level, within easy reach of the gerbils.

This type of drinker ensures that they have a clean supply of fresh water constantly available, whereas an open container in the cage is soon likely to be partially filled with shavings, for example. The bedding material will absorb the water, leaving none for the gerbils, or alternatively, the water may be contaminated by fecal matter.

Gerbils consume only small volumes of water daily, perhaps just 0.2 fl.oz.

(4ml) each, but it should always be available to them. Change this supply daily, and once a week, wash the drinker thoroughly, using a special bottle brush for this purpose. If you add any detergent, you must rinse the drinker to ensure that none remains when you refill it for the gerbils.

The same applies with disinfectants. Remember that since water accumulates between the two valves in the nozzle, you should place this under a running tap, to force out any contaminated water. If you have a large collection of gerbils, housed in cages in close proximity to each other, then you may prefer to use an automatic drinking system for your stock. Running off a central feed, drinking valves are fitted to each cage. Water should only flow out of the valve when the gerbils

Caring for a gerbil can help to promote a child's sense of responsibility and respect for animals. (If youngsters are very young, they should have adult supervision when caring for or playing with their pet.)

apply pressure to the valve, so there should be virtually no leakage.

In addition, check that no backflow is possible in the system. Otherwise disease could be spread from one drinker to another as a result. Choose dark black plastic connecting tubing, since this will prevent algae growing in the interior of the system, as there will be no light present here.

You must also be certain that any build-up of mineral salts, caused by the evaporation of water, will not interfere with the functioning of the individual drinking valves. Greater problems in this regard are likely to result if you opt for a push-button valve system, because the springs are likely to be affected by just a minor build-up here.

You can flush the system every week, and if necessary, follow the manufacturer's instructions about the use of disinfectants, such as chlorine bleach, at regular intervals. The need to disinfect the system will be paramount after the addition of any medication or vitamin solutions to the drinking water.

It can be easier, therefore, to dose one cage by simply using a regular drinking bottle, rather than providing water-born vitamins to all the gerbils in your collection.

VITAMIN AND MINERAL TONICS

Under normal circumstances, gerbils should receive a balanced diet, and the need for additional supplementation is slight. But if you have a convalescing gerbil, then the use of a special tonic can be helpful. Ask at your pet store for the brands which they have available. Aside from tonics added to the water, the more comprehensive supplements of this type are usually produced in powdered form. These can be dispensed easily by being sprinkled over a favorite item of fresh food, such as greenfood or apple.

The powder will stick well to these moist surfaces, especially if they have been washed beforehand and are still damp. Try to persuade the gerbils to take this food from your fingers however, because some will inevitably be lost if it comes into contact with the bedding.

It cannot be stressed too strongly that greenfoods (carrots, lettuce, and the like) should be fed only occasionally and in small portions. Gastrointestinal problems such as diarrhea are likely to occur if you overfeed greenfoods to your pet.

Taming and Handling Gerbils

One of the main reasons for the Mongolian gerbil's popularity as a pet is the ease with which it can be tamed. In turn, gerbils can then give a great deal of pleasure to owners. Small children in particular are often fascinated by these creatures and will learn a great deal about them, both by watching them and actually handling them.

But careful adult supervision is always necessary when the gerbils are out of their cage. Children are not always good judges of their own strength, and an over-affectionate squeeze could prove fatal for the gerbil.

Do not be too worried if your gerbils initially prove rather nervous and shy when you first purchase them. They should soon settle down in their new surroundings and become tame. Try to avoid sudden movements near their cage, which are likely to scare them and set back the taming process.

It may take two or three weeks for your new pets to settle down well with you, depending partly on how much handling they have previously been used to. Although gerbils' naturally inquisitive and friendly character will help the training process enormously, you must win their trust and build up their confidence in you through these early stages.

Give your gerbil time to adjust to his new environment before trying to handtame him.

SETTLING IN AT HOME

Assuming that you have purchased all of your gerbils at the same time, you will simply need to introduce them to their new quarters when you reach home. Prepare everything in advance, so that you will just need to place them straight in their accommodation. At this stage, even strange gerbils which have not been kept together should settle in without any problems of aggression, assuming they are still young.

It is probably a good idea to move them straight to their quarters once you arrive home, although some people prefer to allow them to stay in the traveling box to recover from the journey, leaving them here for an hour or so without disturbance at this stage. Certainly, you should avoid unnecessary handling through the initial period, in case the stress of movement and unfamiliar surroundings induces a case of epilepsy, to which Mongolian gerbils are susceptible.

You might be able to transfer them directly from the traveling box to their new home, simply by opening the doors. If you prop open the door of the main cage, it may be possible to open the door of the traveling box opposite this gap. Especially with food present in their new cage, the gerbils will soon move out to explore these strange surroundings. It is important to ensure that they cannot slip out through any gap into the room, however, when these doors are opened.

Alternatively, if you are using a converted aquarium for housing your gerbils, you may be able to lift the traveling box straight in,

This youngster is holding his pet gerbil in a safe manner. With one hand he has a secure grip on the animal's body; he uses his other hand as a sort of safety cushion.

and allow them to climb out directly into their new home. Failing either of these options, you must otherwise catch the gerbils directly in order to move them. Encourage them to step on to your hand, and avoid grasping them tightly. If you are worried about being bitten at this stage, then wear a thin pair of gloves, moving each gerbil individually.

Above: The first time you hold your gerbil, he may squirm and try to escape from your grip.

Facing page: When handling a gerbil, make every effort not to startle or frighten him.

Having adequate food, water, and bedding, the gerbils should then be left alone for twenty-four hours. It is probably best not to attempt to handle them at all during this period, so they can settle in without additional stress. Once they are used to their surroundings, you can start to tame them. Like all animals, gerbils come to recognize a routine, and it is a good idea to start by feeding them at a set time each day. They will soon get used to this, and await their food eagerly.

In the first few days, simply place the mix in their food pot, once or twice a

day. Move your hand slowly and unhurriedly in the cage, and speak quietly to your new pets as you feed them. Soon they will be far less nervous, as they become used to having your hand in their quarters for short periods.

Your next aim should be to persuade them to feed directly from your hand.

Below: With time and patience, your gerbil will come to accept you—and your handling. **Facing page:** An excellent way to hold a gerbil. Note how the animal is secured at the base of his tail.

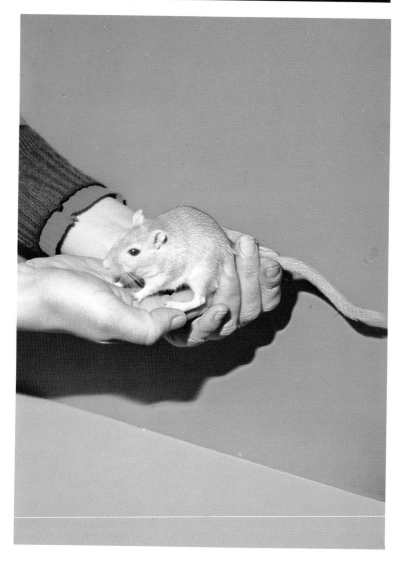

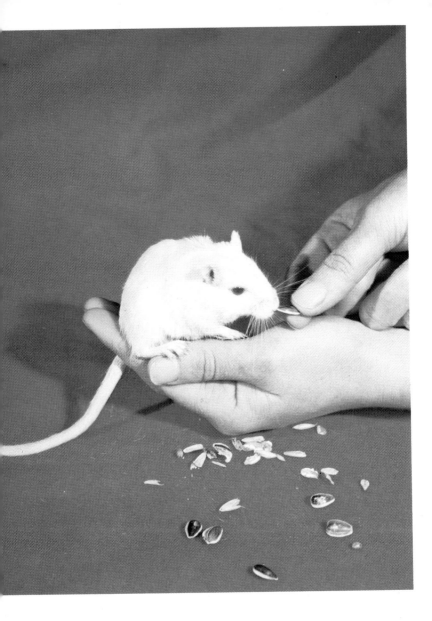

Choose an item of food, such as sunflower seed, which is a favorite of most gerbils. Hold a large seed between your thumb and forefinger, placing your hand slowly in the cage.

You may need to be patient, as the gerbils will probably be reluctant to approach at first. But you should find that their curiosity finally overcomes their natural fear, and they will at least approach your hand, even if they are still reluctant to take the seed. On the first occasion, one of the gerbils is likely to rush forward and grab it, before retreating with equal speed.

If your offering is ignored, then repeat the process later during the day. After five minutes or so, the

Facing page: The taming process can be greatly facilitated by offering your gerbil food rewards. This little fellow seems a bit tentative about nibbling at the seed that his handler is offering him.

gerbils should have taken the offering. Once one has eaten the seed, then repeat the process immediately, to see if its companion can be persuaded to feed from your hand as well.

By repeating this process regularly, you will soon find that the gerbils become progressively less nervous. They readily look forward to receiving the seed and may eat it close to your hand, instead of retreating away from your presence. Make no attempt to touch the gerbils at this stage, and speak softly at all times, so they become used to the sound of your voice.

The next step is to place a small quantity of seed or other tidbits in the palm of your hand. Lower this into the gerbils' quarters, and encourage them to approach your open hand in order to feed. Again, they may dart off at first, but soon they will remain here quite contentedly.

Once things have progressed to this point, you can begin to stroke your pets gently. Start by touching the back and sides of their body, stroking away from the face, following the lie of the fur. Avoid touching the head directly, as this is likely to scare a gerbil which is not yet used to being handled. Soon your gerbils will accept this attention readily, and by this stage, they will already be quite tame.

The final step is to encourage the gerbils to come out of their quarters, so that you can pick them up. This will be easier if they are housed in a cage with a low door, rather than a converted aquarium. In any event, it is important to ensure that your pets are safe when they are in the room.

You must be sure to exclude your other pets, notably cats and dogs, which could harm the gerbils, and keep the door closed, so that they will not be able to escape outside the room. It is a good idea to let only one gerbil out at a time, so you can supervise it properly.

Start by placing the cage on a large, flat, firm surface, such as a table. Open the door, and then resting your hand on the table some inches away, wait for the gerbil to emerge. Keep the gerbil's favorite food clearly visible in the palm of your hand as further encouragement.

Then, when it has been feeding confidently, you can stroke it as usual. Once it is out of its quarters, watch it

Facing page: Some gerbils can be more skittish than others. If you know your pet to be of this type of nature, you must take extra precautions to hold him securely.

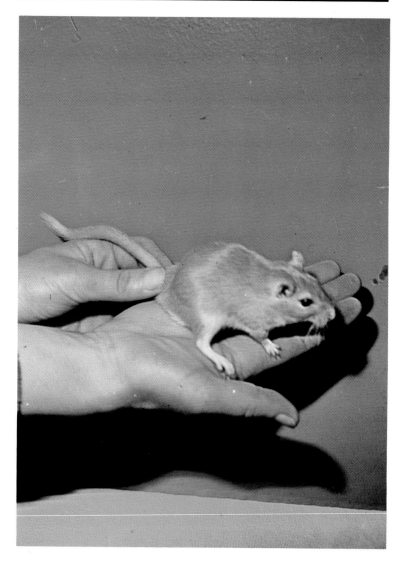

carefully. Gerbils often show no sense of heights and could easily fall if allowed to run near the edge of the table.

The situation will be different with gerbils housed in a converted aquarium, as you will then need to lift each one out in turn. Always restrain a gerbil first by the base of its tail, close to the junction with the body, and avoid the fragile tip of the tail. Your grip should be firm but not tight, as you lift your pet, restraining it carefully between the thumb and fingers of the other hand.

By holding the base of the tail, you are limiting the gerbil's ability to wriggle and possibly bite and escape from your grasp. As always, ensure that your movements are steady, and speak softly to your pet. It will soon become used to being handled and may eventually be sufficiently tame to sit freely on your hand or run up your arm.

Under no circumstances whatsoever should you attempt to restrain the gerbil by the tip of its tail. The skin here is loose and easily damaged. It will then bleed readily, and in some cases, the tip may actually be lost as a result if the injury is severe.

You must also obviously avoid holding a gerbil upside down, even if you are supporting its body in your hand, for any length of time; this could trigger an epileptic fit.

Finally, until it is extremely tame and used to handling, do not attempt to

Facing page: When holding your gerbil, use a firm but not tight grip, and always hold him right side up.

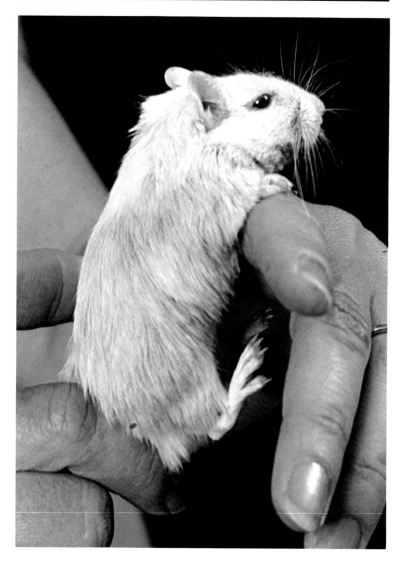

pick the gerbil up on your closed hand. Always restrain it first by the base of the tail. Gentle and careful handling from an early age should ensure that your pet does not bite you.

In the case of exhibition gerbils, it is also important that they are easily handled if they are to impress the judge at shows. This aspect must not be neglected in the larger stud, therefore, even though there may be less time to spend on each individual gerbil.

Above: This youngster is carefully watching his gerbil being examined by a judge at a gerbil show. Young people especially enjoy the fun and excitement of showing their pets.

Facing page: Even the most tame gerbil might try to jump out of his owner's hand. If this happens to you, remember that a food treat can be used to lure the animal back to you.

ESCAPES

If your gerbil escapes and disappears into the room while out of its cage, you should be able to recapture it without too much difficulty, provided that you are patient. Trying to grab at it is unlikely to prove successful. In the first place, be sure that the door of the room is kept closed, as are windows, so that your pet cannot escape further afield.

Then rely on its natural curiosity and hunger. Place a favorite food and a little bedding in the bottom of a straight-sided plastic kitchen bucket. Construct a series of steps up to the top, using a secure stack of books, or better still, a ramp with a piece of shelving.

Leave the room quietly, and then probably at night, the gerbil's explorations will lead it to try and reach the food. It will climb up the ramp, and drop into the bucket, from where it should not be able to escape again. In the morning, you can then return it to its quarters.

If you see the gerbil, you

This gerbil and mouse are obviously used to each other's company. Such a relationship can come about if the animals are raised together from a young age.

can use an alternative method to recapture it, provided that you have a cage with a spring-loaded door. Attach a piece of cord to this, and be sure that there is food available in the cage. Then hopefully, the gerbil will be attracted inside to feed, at which point you must release your grip on the cord. The door should then shut immediately, leaving the gerbil back within its cage. Obviously, when you have two or more together, the other individuals will need to be removed to secure quarters if you are using this method, because otherwise they may escape as well while the door is open!

TOYS FOR GERBILS

Tame gerbils lose their natural shyness and will be interested in what is going on in the room around them, but they also benefit from the provision of toys in their quarters.

Allowing your gerbils to play with plastic toys, such as those designed for parakeets, is not advisable. If the gerbils swallow pieces of plastic, these are likely to cause problems in the digestive tract, while any sharp pieces of metal exposed as a result of their gnawing activities could lead to serious injury to the gerbils' mouth, at the very least.

Some manufacturers produce special toys for gerbils, and these are obviously to be recommended, being designed specially to meet their needs. Wooden gnaws in various shapes are both attractive and useful toys for gerbils. They will help to keep the incisor teeth in shape, preventing them from becoming overgrown.

But under no circumstances should you give your gerbils the kind of playwheel sold for mice and hamsters, with gaps

Keep in mind that gerbils can vary in the degree to which they can be tamed. Some gerbils are simply more receptive to human contact than are others.

between the treads. A gerbil's tail is not prehensile like that of a mouse—it cannot be kept out of these gaps voluntarily.

As a result, if a gerbil uses a playwheel of this type, then its tail is very likely to become trapped between the gap as the wheel spins. At the very least, this is likely to result in the thin covering of fur and skin being stripped away, while

Above and facing page: Even though the plastic toys shown here appear sturdy, they can be subject to damage because of the gerbil's extraordinary ability to gnaw virtually anything. Additionally, if a gerbil ingests bits of plastic, he could be subject to serious digestive problems.

Your pet shop dealer can best advise you on the types of cage accessories that are most suitable for your gerbil.

at worst, there is a very real risk that the tail will actually be broken off.

Gerbils are not as keen on playwheels as are hamsters, but if you do want to provide them with a toy of this type, then choose a continuous closed plastic wheel with a fully enclosed back. There will be no gaps where your pet could injure itself.

You may decide to provide a hamster-type house where the gerbils can sleep. Various designs are available, and again, it will be safest to avoid any with open-rung ladders as part of their design. Fairly spacious housing of this type is to be recommended, and it should be lined with some snug nesting material.

Some household objects can also be provided as playthings for your gerbils. Examples include clean wooden cotton-reels (obviously with no cotton attached), and cardboard tubing. The latter item is especially popular, being used as tunnels, and also for gnawing purposes.

HOUSEKEEPING

Gerbils are very clean and do not have an unpleasant odor associated with them. But their quarters must be cleaned

Even though gerbils are noted for being relatively clean animals, it is necessary that their cages be cleaned on a regular basis. Good gerbil husbandry can help to keep your stock healthy.

regularly and thoroughly to ensure they remain in good health. It is preferable to move the gerbils to an alternate temporary accommodation for this period. A cheap plastic fish tank is ideal for this purpose.

You can then discard the

Proper maintenance of your gerbil's living quarters also includes the removal of all chew items that are worn down.

old bedding and wash out the gerbils' quarters if necessary. Allow the base to dry thoroughly before putting in clean bedding and replacing the toys. If for any reason you have used a disinfectant, it is particularly important that you rinse the unit to remove any traces, as these residues could subsequently prove harmful to the gerbils.

You should be able to purchase special safe disinfectants formulated for use in pet accommodations from your local pet store. As always with chemicals, follow the instructions for use carefully when making up the solution.

If you are keeping the gerbils in a clear acrylic tank, bear in mind that using very hot water to wash it out is likely to cause the plastic to become opaque, restricting the visibility of your pets as a result. It is also very easy to scratch the sides, so try to remove as much debris as possible while the tank is dry, before wiping out the interior with a damp cloth.

With a metal cage, avoid washing it more than absolutely necessary, since this may encourage the development of rust and shorten its lifespan as a result. Never be tempted to use any metal polish on the bars of the cage, because this is very likely to prove toxic, should the gerbils start to nibble at the bars.

Once the bars are showing signs of rust, it is preferable to obtain a new cage. If the gerbils ingest the rust particles, these can otherwise damage their sensitive digestive tract. But provided that you take care of the cage and provide adequate bedding so that the floor cannot become saturated, then it should certainly suffice for the lifespan of the gerbils.

After you have cleaned your gerbil's cage, remember that the animal cannot be put back into it until it is thoroughly dry. Keeping a gerbil in a damp environment can make it ill.

Breeding Gerbils

Assuming that you enjoy keeping your gerbils, then sooner or later, you will probably want to breed them. This decision, however, needs to be considered carefully, especially as it is likely to involve an input of both greater time and expense on your part. You must consider the future of any litters produced—can you keep the offspring if no one else wants them?

This applies especially if you are intending to breed gerbils on a regular basis for exhibition purposes. You are then certain to produce more youngsters than you will want to retain, as your stud develops. You will be aiming to produce gerbils which conform as closely as possible to the standard or ideal for the variety concerned. Although other breeders may well be willing to purchase some good quality offspring, you will inevitably be left with youngsters which, although healthy, are not suitable for exhibition purposes. You will have to find good homes for these animals. An advertisement in a local paper may be a means of achieving this aim.

BREEDING BEHAVIOR

In the wild, gerbils usually live in colonies numbering up to 30 to 40 animals. Within this group, a social hierarchy is established, with dominant males and females. Each male has his own territory and partner. He will fight any other male who attempts to mate with her, and she in turn resists the

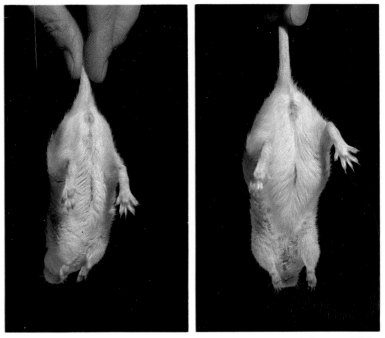

Sexing a gerbil is done by examining the animal's genital area. (This position is very uncomfortable—and potentially injurious—for them so this procedure should be carried out as quickly as possible.)

attentions of any male lower in the social structure of the group.

By this means, the strongest and fittest animals pair together, with natural selection ensuring that the colony produces the best possible offspring to parent the next generation. This has several implications for the gerbil breeder, not least the fact that if only a few animals are kept, then the

A dove gerbil and an agouti Canadian white spot gerbil pictured during mating.

natural hierarchy cannot develop. As a result, it becomes the keeper's task to select the strongest and healthiest animals to mate together.

In addition, the natural antagonism which exists between strong adult gerbils can create problems when trying to pair two individuals which may nevertheless have desirable characteristics of color and shape. As a result, there is a considerable advantage in pairing young animals that have not reached sexual maturity. They will then accept each other readily as partners, and mate without problems in due course.

Young gerbils reach sexual maturity between nine and twelve weeks of age, but will not necessarily mate immediately at this stage. If they do so, the first litter may be very small and might be ignored by the female. If these offspring are neglected, this should not be taken as a sign that she will prove to be a poor mother in the future.

During the 15 to 20 months of her reproductive life, a female gerbil is likely to produce about seven litters, with an average of about six youngsters per litter, so that she should not be discarded from your breeding program on the basis of one early failure.

The female's period of heat, or estrus, when she is receptive to mating and likely to conceive, lasts for about four days and recurs with a gap of six days between each period. Mating itself is very brief, but takes place frequently, most commonly during the early evening.

Initially, the male will pursue the female around the cage. When she is ready, she will stop running and

This male agouti gerbil and argente female gerbil are being introduced for the first time. Gerbils are prolific breeders...Will you be able to keep and care for the youngsters if no one else wants them?

adopts the mating stance, allowing the male to mount her. She then resumes running around the cage, followed by the male who frequently washes himself after mating, before repeating the process again.

Once her period of heat has past, the female will not accept the male's attentions.

If you are trying to pair up two adults, this can be a problem, as they may fight, especially if the female is not in heat. You will therefore need to supervise the mating carefully, taking steps to avoid any outbreak of hostility between the partners.

Start by using a neutral cage, which neither animal will have established as its own territory. You may

Above: The breeding cage should be neutral; that is, neither the male nor the female should have established it as their own territory.

Facing page: A black female gerbil and her one-day-old babies.

decide to fit a wire mesh partition, which you can remove once the two gerbils appear to have accepted each other. Should you have no option but to introduce one to the other's territory, then it is preferable to allow the male to be the host to the female, and not vice-versa.

Once the pair are first placed together, watch very carefully, and be ready to intervene as soon as any evident fighting begins. Repeating the introductory process later may lead to a less aggressive encounter, especially if the female is then in heat.

At first, the gerbils are likely to circle each other continuously, sniffing at their ventral areas to establish each other's gender. If they are to be immediately compatible, they will simply circle and sniff several times, and display no signs of

aggression. If no fighting has taken place after some 10 or 15 minutes, you can leave them together reasonably safely, without further worry.

In most cases, however, it is more likely that the sniffing will be followed by the gerbils' drumming their heels and locking their teeth. If the female then decides to submit, she will drop down, lying slightly on her side, holding her head to explore his throat. The male will probably then respond by licking her face. Again, once this stage has been reached, there is a good possibility that there will be no further signs of aggression.

You will need to act rapidly, however, if the locking of teeth is followed by a full-scale fight. Gerbils can injure each other quite seriously unless separated without delay, and might even fight to the death. Be

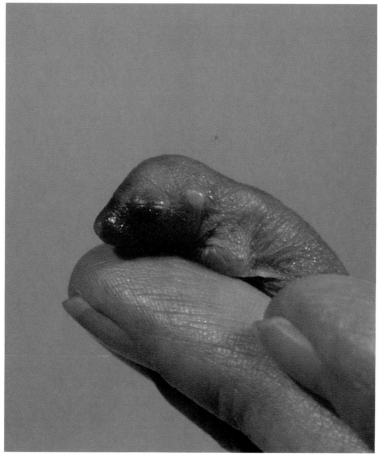

A pallid gerbil several hours old. Features such as the ears and eyes are clearly visible.

sure to have a stout pair of leather gardening gloves available, in case you need to part the animals. Otherwise you could be badly bitten or scratched without such protection, when separating the animals.

The most direct method is simply to place your hands between them, removing one of the combatants to separate quarters.

Below and facing page: A pair of pallid gerbils and their young. The gestation period for gerbils is about 25 days in duration.

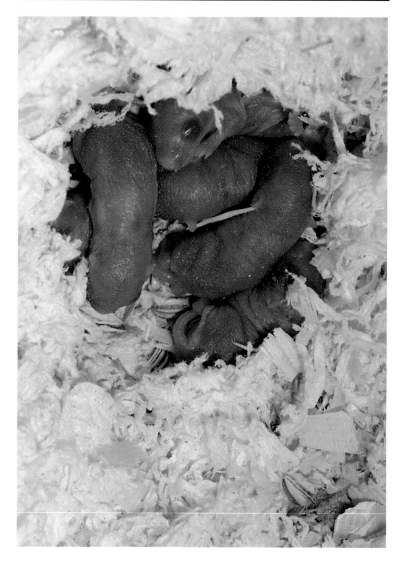

Alternatively, you can use a stout, flat piece of wood to divide them, and then transfer them back by hand to their individual cages without delay. Rapid action will prevent any serious injury which could ruin the show potential of exhibition stock.

Following such a fight, allow four or five days to elapse before trying to introduce the gerbils again. It may well be that after this interval, the female is in heat and more likely to be receptive to the male. If the pairing is important, then be patient. You will need to be prepared to give the gerbils several opportunities to accept each other.

Should repeated introductions fail, you may be able to overcome their resistance to each other by dusting them with talcum powder. This acts as a masking agent, disguising their individual scents, so

that fighting is less likely to arise. But should this method prove unsuccessful, it is probably best to abandon this mating, and try them each with a different partner.

Some strains may be naturally more aggressive than others, and since such aggression could be an inherited trait, it may be better to concentrate on developing your bloodlines from essentially compatible stock. Gerbils which are known to have strong fighting tendencies are best excluded from your breeding program if possible.

Once a pair of gerbils have accepted each other, the bond between them is very strong. If left together, they will mate for life. This does not, however, preclude them from being mated successfully with others, as may well be necessary in an

A young gerbil attempting to leave the nest. Gerbils are born without fur, and their eyes are closed. At approximately two weeks of age, their eyes open.

exhibition stud. But reintroductions will also need to be carried out carefully as well.

PREGNANCY AND BIRTH

The gestation period, which is another way of describing the length of the female's pregnancy, lasts approximately 25 days. At first, there will be no obvious external signs, but gradually, you will notice that her abdomen is beginning to swell, and by the end of the pregnancy, her normal body weight will have doubled.

If mating took place in a special or neutral cage, then the female should be moved soon afterwards to the quarters where the young will be born. Some hobbyists prefer to separate the pregnant gerbil from her mate; others do not.

Feed the pregnant female and her mate as usual, but as her pregnancy advances, it can be beneficial to provide additional greenfood and use a food supplement. Ensure that plenty of water is available, but avoid overfeeding her with fatty foods such as sunflower seeds. This may potentially lead to her experiencing difficulties in giving birth later.

You may decide to provide a budgerigar (parakeet) nestbox on the floor of the quarters, so the female can have additional seclusion when giving birth. But in most cases, there is no need, with the usual bedding enabling the mother to prepare a perfectly adequate nest.

Try to give her quarters a very good clean before the litter is due, so as to minimize any disturbance soon after the young are born. Do not handle the

A pallid gerbil mother with her young. Baby gerbils are totally helpless at birth and totally depend on their mother for food, warmth, and protection.

female more than necessary however, especially during these latter stages of pregnancy.

The birth itself is most likely to take place at night, and the female will cope with it quite easily by herself. The young, which measure about one-half inch (1.25cm) long, are born naked and blind, with no teeth evident and their ears sealed. At this stage, they are totally dependent on their mother for food, warmth, and protection. She will spend most of her time in the nest with them, leaving them only very briefly in order to feed or drink.

Although it is exceedingly tempting to see and count the litter, try to avoid disturbing the nest, at least for the first three or four days. So long as the babies' high-pitched squeaking can be heard,

you can assume that all is progressing quite well. After this stage, you may wish to inspect the youngsters cautiously, removing any which have died in the nest, although this is not common. The problem is most likely to arise with females giving birth for the first time, and in the case of abnormally large litters.

The safest method for inspecting the nest is to first distract the mother from her offspring by offering her a special tidbit. Then remove her (and the tidbit) to another cage out of sight from the nest. Take a clean plastic straw, and rub it for a few moments in the litter of her usual quarters, so that it loses its own scent, and resembles that of the gerbils. You should avoid handling it more than necessary in the first instance, so that the straw does not acquire your scent.

If at all possible, try to avoid handling the baby gerbils until they leave their nest—at about ten days of age. If for some reason the young must be handled before this time, rub some litter over your hands to camouflage your own scent and to avoid upsetting the mother.

Use the straw very gently to part the nesting material so that you can see the youngsters within the nest. It should be possible to remove a dead youngster using the straw to move it clear of the nest in the first instance, before removing it by hand or with forceps. In any event, re-cover the nest as quickly as possible and return the mother, perhaps rewarding her again with a sunflower seed or similar treat.

Apart from this brief inspection, the litter should be left entirely alone until the youngsters emerge from the nest of their own accord at about ten days old. One or two may be seen earlier than this, if their mother does not detach them from her nipples when she herself comes out to feed. Should this happen, it is not usually necessary to intervene, because she will return them to the nest.

If you do need to handle the young gerbils before they are independent, again rub your hands in the nest litter first, so that you have the scent of their mother on your hands. Then, after touching them, this will help

The average litter size for a gerbil is about five youngsters. Thus, this litter is a bit on the small side. Gerbil pups (babies) have a birth weight of about three grams.

This photo illustrates just how tiny baby gerbils are. At birth, they are less than one inch in body length.

to disguise any unfamiliar scent on the offspring when she returns to them.

Young gerbils develop quite quickly after birth. Their skin will turn from pink to a darkish coloration within three or four days, and then a week after birth, a very light coat of fur will have appeared. At seven to ten days old, their ears will be developed and opened, and by this stage the young gerbils are about an inch (2.5cm) in length. By two weeks old, their teeth will begin to emerge, and their eyes start to open.

The youngsters are more adventurous by this stage, leaving the nest of their own

accord. Both parents will now supervise them, returning them here at intervals. After a further week or so, the young gerbils will be complete miniature versions of their parents. They should appear extremely active when awake, squabbling and playing, even climbing over the adults.

The weaning process will now be well underway, as the youngsters will have started taking solid foods at about two and a half weeks old. They will begin to discover food quite naturally, by playing with and sampling bits of their parents' food. Initially, the young gerbils may be unable to crack seeds, for example, but they soon

Facing page: The physical development rate of gerbils is truly remarkable. This baby gerbil will be fully mature and ready for breeding at approximately twelve weeks of age.

learn to develop the necessary skills to enable themselves to feed independently.

When they are between three and four weeks old, (unless you keep your gerbils on the colony system), you should separate offspring from their parents. By this stage, the adult female could well be pregnant again. She might have mated successfully within a day of giving birth, although should this happen, it seems that the fertilized eggs do not immediately implant into the wall of the uterus. This delay causes the gestation period to be prolonged as a result.

At approximately one month old, once sexing is straightforward, you may also choose to separate males and females from a litter, so they do not form pair bonds with each other.

Now is a good time to place them with other partners, and part with any of the youngsters which are surplus to your future breeding plans.

The point of separation from their parents is an important one for the young. They should be watched very carefully at this stage for any signs of ill health or disinterest in food. Any gerbil which is not

Above: A litter of two-week-old gerbils. As they mature, their tails will lengthen and thus will be more in proportion to their bodies.

Facing page: Two-week-old gerbil. Note the glossy quality of its coat.

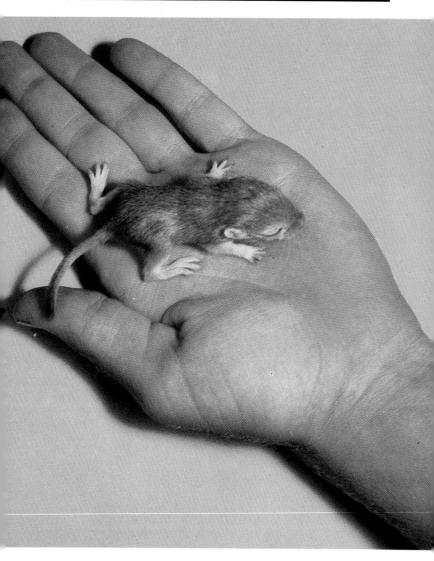

eating properly will soon appear dull and depressed, behaving lethargically. It will become rather fluffed up in appearance.

You may even need to return such a youngster to its parents for a further period. If it has only recently been removed, then they will usually accept it back without problems. But to reinforce their scent, you may want to rub its fur gently with bedding from their quarters beforehand.

DEALING WITH PROBLEMS

The majority of young gerbils are reared to maturity without difficulties, but on occasion, problems may arise which require your attention. Avoid creating unnecessary disturbance yourself. At any time when you need to touch or examine the youngsters while they are

with their parents, you should always take the precaution of running your fingers through the litter on the cage floor first, to mask your scent. This is particularly important with a nervous mother, because if she detects a strange smell associated with her offspring, she may desert, or, even worse, destroy them.

Should young be left unattended, usually because the mother dies during the rearing period, you may be able to foster them successfully onto another female, if you have a sufficiently large stock with a number of females breeding simultaneously. Under these circumstances, start by removing the intended foster mother from her nest as described previously. Then place the new babies with the original offspring so that they take on the scent of the foster family.

You can encourage the female to accept the newcomers by then sprinkling wheat germ over the fur of the babies. Once she is returned to her nest, the mother will be distracted by this. It will encourage her to clean all the youngsters, and as a result, she will cover every one with her scent, making the newcomers' acceptance more likely.

Try to introduce gerbils of a similar age, assuming you have any option when fostering them, and avoid adding a large number to the litter of a single female. It is advisable to divide a large group of babies

This mother gerbil keeps a watchful eye over her sleeping babies. Even though it is tempting, try to avoid overhandling the youngsters.

between two foster mothers. This increases the likelihood of all the offspring being reared successfully, without overtaxing a particular female.

CONTROLLED BREEDING

When the time comes for separating them from their parents, it may sometimes be easier if the adult gerbils, rather than their offspring, are moved to new accommodation. This can make the weaning period less traumatic.

Obviously, if they are being housed as a colony, then no separation will be necessary, at least with the first litter, but eventually, you will need to remove some animals.

Gerbils will, to a certain

A litter of three-week-old gerbil youngsters at play. In general, gerbil babies appear to be as hardy as adult gerbils.

extent, regulate their own numbers when housed in such surroundings. Their reproductive activity usually declines once their environment starts to become overcrowded. You can also contribute to reducing their numbers and future litters by separating the young into single sex groups and housing them elsewhere.

BREEDING RECORDS

One important aspect of breeding which must not be forgotten is the keeping of accurate records. Of course, if you have just a small number of gerbils as pets, you may not want to bother. In addition, if they are being kept on the colony system, then record-keeping is pointless, because you cannot be absolutely certain of the paternity of any particular litter.

But for the serious breeder and exhibition enthusiast, absolute accuracy is essential. This will enable color and physical characteristics to be mapped out, valuable qualities retained and improved, while poor ones can be discarded through a careful breeding program.

A card index system provides a straightforward means of record-keeping, with each individual animal being allocated a card bearing its date of birth, details of its parents and grandparents (at the very least), its coloration or other identifying features. Also on the card, you can cross-reference this individual to its siblings.

If each gerbil is given a name or a number, this information can be used to identify it both within the card index, and also within the stud. A code showing the identification number,

When selecting gerbils for your breeding program, it is essential to choose animals that are healthy and hardy.

color and date of birth of the individual concerned should also be fixed to its cage.

You should keep your records on each animal as up-to-date as possible. For ease of access to the information, you may want to have a separate studbook as well, where you can include further details. Breeding information, such as the dates of birth for litters, the number of individuals per litter, litter size, and any losses of young during the rearing period can prove very useful as examples.

When a gerbil dies or leaves your stud, this should also be recorded on the card index. You may want to place a black spot or star at the top right hand side of the cards of such individuals, to identify the fact they are no longer in the stud. But information about their parentage and descendants could be useful for the future, so do not discard their records immediately.

BREEDING SYSTEMS

With accurate pedigrees available, you can pair the gerbils to give the greatest opportunity of producing top quality offspring. Various breeding systems can be used for this purpose. These are described as crossbreeding, linebreeding, and inbreeding.

In the first instance, you will probably start by mating unrelated gerbils,

which is known as crossbreeding. The resulting offspring may or may not be "quality" animals, with characteristics superior to their parents. By selecting the best of these youngsters, you may then decide to pair gerbils which are somewhat related together, in an attempt to fix and improve still further on these strengths in the next generation.

Linebreeding can involve the breeding of aunt or uncle to cousin, cousin to cousin, or half-sister to half-brother. By this means, a loss of vitality and strength is less likely, while it is still possible to concentrate desirable characteristics in the emerging strain.

Inbreeding is the process of mating animals that are much more closely-related, for example: mother to son, father to daughter, or brother to sister. The need for good record-keeping is very apparent if this type of breeding system is being applied.

When inbreeding is practiced over several generations, the relationships can become quite complex, with one male, for example, being both father and grandfather to one individual. This can be easily understood if we call the male "A" and his first mate "B." Their daughter, known as "C," is then mated back to her father, producing another young female, "D."

If "D" is then mated with "A," the resulting litter will have "A" as both father and grandfather. Such breeding systems are useful in fixing good points of body and color in stock which is already of a high standard, but you will need to select from the offspring very carefully to retain only those which exceed their parents in the desired qualities. Otherwise, the risk remains of introducing and selectively concentrating faults, which will then become very difficult to eradicate from your stock.

Inbreeding cannot be carried on indefinitely in any event. Sooner or later, a strain of gerbils that has been consistently inbred will show signs of weakness, such as a regular decrease in litter sizes or declining physical qualities.

Before this point is reached, an animal from a totally different strain, known as an "outcross," must be introduced. It should excel in the weaker points of the established strain, rather than simply complementing its strengths. Outcrossing gives fresh blood and the opportunity to refine the bloodline still further, before a

Inbreeding enables the hobbyist to fix and improve desired characteristics in his stock.

deterioration in the stud occurs.

GENETICS

If you are interested in breeding gerbils of a particular color, then you will need to consider the laws of inheritance. These were first formulated during the mid 19th century by Gregor Mendel, an Austrian monk. Based on a study of pea plants, he recognized inherited characteristics which were passed from one generation to the next. These ensured that the offspring displayed the same essential characteristics as their parents.

Twentieth century research has unraveled the mysteries of this inheritance system even further. It has discovered the cell nucleus contained within each female egg and male sperm, the thread-like

chromosomes within each cell nucleus, and the genes, the minute bodies on the chromosomes which actually convey the individual inherited characteristics directly from one generation to the next.

The number of chromosomes remains constant from one generation to the next, ensuring that gerbils result. But the precise details of the individual's fur color, eye color, body shape, and so on will depend on the information carried in the genes in each pair of chromosomes. This method ensures that individual genetic characteristics can be subtly shifted or rearranged in each succeeding generation.

It might, therefore, appear that the offspring will show a mixture of their parents' characteristics, but this is not inevitably the case, because some genes are dominant over others, and these in turn will dictate the actual appearance of the offspring. Genes can thus be basically divided into "dominant" or "recessive" forms.

As a consequence, it is also important to realize that although two gerbils may appear identical in terms of their appearance, (known technically as having the same phenotype), their genetic constitution (or genotype) may be quite different. It is this genetic information which will be passed on to their offspring, and these are likely to differ in appearance as a result.

Where there are two identical genes, either dominant or recessive, on the paired chromosomes, the individual is sometimes described as being homozygous for that particular characteristic. But if the genes are different, with one being dominant and the other recessive, then that gerbil is known as heterozygous, or more commonly, "split" for the recessive characteristic.

While this may seem rather baffling terminology, the following practical examples will clarify the situation and explain the significance of these genetic differences. To simplify their descriptions for this purpose, the gerbil color forms are given a letter code. The dominant gene is given a capital letter, while the recessive is indicated by a lower case letter.

The natural color of the Mongolian gerbil is described as agouti and is dominant, so it is coded as "A." The pink-eyed white characteristic, being recessive, can be shown as "w." The following breeding

A successful breeding program requires a basic knowledge of genetics.

situation could then arise.

A pure-bred agouti male, whose ancestors for many past generations were also agouti, is therefore called AA (with one gene on each of the two chromosomes). When mated with a pink-eyed white, all their offspring will be Aw.

The agouti gene is dominant to that of the pink-eyed white, and so the youngsters appear agouti in color, but also have a "hidden" pink-eyed white gene as part of their genotype. This is because they receive genes from both of their parents.

The pink-eyed white characteristic may then reappear in some of the offspring in the next (F2) generation. If, for example, two Aw gerbils from the original F1 pairing mate together, then some of them will inherit just agouti (A) genes from their parents,

and others just pink-eyed white (w) genes. But a significant number will acquire one agouti (A) gene and one pink-eyed white (w) gene.

Statistically, the most likely outcome is 25 percent pure agouti (AA); 25 percent pure pink-eyed white (ww); and 50 percent agouti/pink-eyed white (Aw), like the parents. The symbol "/" indicates a heterozygous combination, with the recessive character always being written after the oblique line.

But since the combination of genes occurs entirely by random, then the exact proportions of the youngsters is likely to vary, on the basis of one or two pairings. In effect, predictions of this type are averages, rather than absolutely precise guidelines in every individual instance.

Many gerbil hobbyists consider breeding for color to be one of the most exciting aspects of the hobby.

THE APPEARANCE OF MUTATIONS

Every so often, again at random, a mutant gene will emerge, particularly in stock that has been closely inbred.

This is a gene which produces a variation on the normal or expected physical characteristics, including coat coloration.

Mutations are most likely

to become established through captive-breeding. This is because in the wild, most mutations are likely to prove less likely to survive than the existing form. For example, a pink-eyed white gerbil would almost certainly be more conspicuous to predators, and could possibly suffer more from heat, because of its coat coloration. Its pink eyes may also be less effective in detecting danger.

Should it manage to survive to maturity, then it will need to pair with a pure-bred agouti, which will be the dominant color in the colony. The results will be identical to those given in the genetics section above: all the offspring will be agouti in appearance, but split for the pink-eyed white characteristic as well. Only in the second generation, therefore, are pink-eyed white gerbils likely to be produced.

In the wild, the likelihood of heterozygotes breeding together is much less than it is in captivity. This is because, with the Mendelian Laws of Inheritance, breeders can set up pairings which will maximize the numbers of heterozygotes and mutant offspring that can be produced. By such careful nurturing, mutations can easily be established in a relatively short space of time.

When a mutant gene first appears, the value of accurate breeding records becomes clear. It is important to be able to track its likely original occurrence and possibly heterozygous individuals still in your collection. These can then be used in a concerted breeding program to develop it through future generations.

Mongolian Gerbil Colors

The natural coloration of the Mongolian gerbil is a rich golden brown with black tips to the fur of the upperparts, while the fur on the undersurface of the body is white. The tail is also somewhat sandy, with a streak of black along the upper side, and a more prominent black tuft at its tip.

Sometimes also described as the white-bellied agouti, the agouti golden, or simply the normal, good exhibition gerbils of this form show a clear division between their light underside and darker coloration above. In a top quality individual, you will be able to see a thin area of golden hairs, with no dark markings evident as a border.

Color mutations of the

Mongolian gerbils. This is the gerbil species with which people are most familiar and which is easiest to obtain.

Mongolian gerbil are all relatively recent in origin. The combination of two primary mutations then creates color forms, and opens up a whole new area for breeders.

The first known gerbil mutation was reported from Canada in the late 1960s. Here it was originally christened the white spot. Such gerbils have the usual agouti coloration over their back and sides, contrasting with slate-gray belly fur. Distinctive white spots are visible, often on the forehead and over the nape of the neck, even occasionally on the tail.

At first, this variety proved quite difficult to establish and was initially found only in the hands of experienced breeders, but it is now more widely available.

A separate variety, although not genetically distinct, is the patched. This has been developed from the white spot. Patched gerbils have more widespread patches of white fur, even along the tail, rather than discrete spots. It is important in either case— white spot or patched—that these gerbils have well-defined white spots or patches.

Interestingly, this particular mutation is dominant to the normal, which means that you can anticipate white spot offspring in the first generation, if you pair a gerbil of this type to an agouti. But there is a lethal factor associated with the mutation, and this means that the litter size is often smaller than normal.

Facing page: The gerbil's capability to produce healthy and uniform young is already established, but its breeding performance is still rather unpredictable.

Above and facing page: Argente gerbil mother and her youngster at play. Argentes are fancied by many hobbyists because of their particularly attractive coloration.

It is impossible to predict the pattern or extent of the spots in the young gerbils. Even if two well-matched white spots are paired together, then their offspring may have little or no spotting evident. In

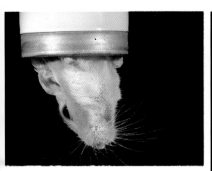

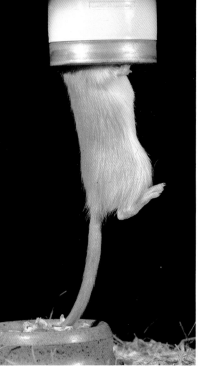

addition, the extent of the spotting also depends on the color variety concerned. Both agouti and argente forms tend to have smaller spotting than in the case of self varieties such as the black. In all cases, however, the basic ground coloration of the variety is unaffected.

Breeders have attempted to standardize the pattern of spotting, but inevitably, a number of otherwise healthy gerbils will not show the necessary markings. Well-defined, circular, even-size spots on the nose, forehead, nape of the neck and rump are deemed generally desirable, with the feet also being white. Right at the tip of the tail, a white spot should also be evident.

Markings for members of the self group are somewhat similar, but generally larger in size, becoming diamond-shaped over the belly. Breeders are endeavoring to increase the size of these white areas, to produce black and white gerbils for example.

BLACK

An American mutation, the black was first bred at the United States Air Force School of Aerospace

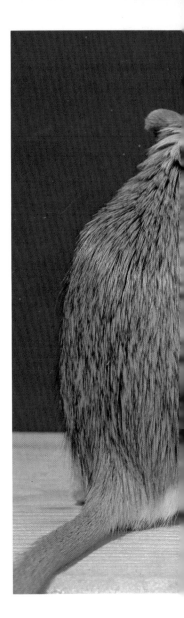

Facing page: An agouti Canadian white spot and a dove gerbil at play.

Medicine, Texas. During the late 1970s, a number were sent to Europe, but proved difficult to establish there, because of the widespread inbreeding in the stock which had taken place previously. Outcrossing with unrelated gerbils was carried out to improve the vitality of this new mutation, and stock is now quite widely-kept.

It is not uncommon to have blacks showing traces of white hairs, but ideally, they should be pure black, with matching eyes, ears and claws. Those with white areas on the throat and feet are frowned upon by exhibition enthusiasts specializing in this mutation.

In addition to obtaining a desired color, gerbil breeders strive to breed animals that are sound, healthy, and of good conformation.

A black female gerbil and an agouti Canadian white spot male gerbil. Both animals are fairly young.

PINK-EYED WHITE

The origins of this popular mutation are unclear, although it was first recorded about 1970. It was first thought to be an albino, but it is *not* a pure red-eyed white without color pigment. In fact, although pink-eyed whites are white at birth, dark-colored hairs become evident along the tail and at the tips of the ears, nose, and feet.

This is the typical so-called Himalayan patterning, recognized in other forms of fancy livestock from mice to cats. The darker guard hairs usually start to become apparent from the age of about three months onwards.

These particular gerbils are relatively slow to mature and may not start breeding until they are at least six months old. Selective pairings are being

undertaken by some breeders to try to deepen the Himalayan patterning. By similar means, it is hoped to develop a virtually pure red-eyed albino strain, lacking the traces of dark markings presently associated with the pink-eyed white.

"GRAY AGOUTI" OR CHINCHILLA

This mutation, at first confused with the pattern known as chinchilla in other small mammals, is a good example of the strange, unexpected way that different colors can suddenly appear. The first gerbil recognized as a "gray agouti" was discovered entirely by chance in a London pet store in 1975.

The black gerbil, which was first bred in the U.S., is now commonly kept by gerbil fanciers everywhere.

Above: A silver gerbil and a white gerbil. **Facing page:** A dove gerbil and a cinnamon gerbil. Even if you are primarily interested in breeding for a particular color, you should still select stock that is of sound health and good quality.

Until more research is done on the color genetics of gerbils, developing a desired color strain is, to a considerable degree, a matter of trial and error.

A blue female gerbil.

This gerbil, a male, went on to win the Best in Show award at the London Championship that year, but died without breeding successfully.

Since the origins of this unique animal were unknown, it seemed that the "gray agouti" might have been lost forever, as no related stock was available in the hope of recreating it. The only possible cause for optimism was that chinchilla, a mutation very similar to the pattern shown by the unique 1975 gerbil, is recognized as a fairly common mutation in other small mammals, including mice and hamsters. It could therefore recur in gerbils before too long.

In 1980, such hopes were apparently realized when a pair of gerbils seemingly of the chinchilla pattern were obtained from a laboratory. Although they themselves did not breed together successfully, the mutation was preserved and developed by pairing each to a pink-eyed white. The resulting offspring were agouti in color, but when paired together, youngsters of a chinchilla-type color appeared in the litters, so the mutation was established.

It is clear, however, that this mutation does not represent the typical chinchilla mutation, because if it were really the true chinchilla, pairing with pink-eyed whites should have yielded further chinchillas. It is probably better, therefore, to not use the name chinchilla for the "gray agouti" mutant until such time as typical

Facing page: Some people feel that the more recent color mutations in gerbils are not as hardy as the long-established agouti gerbil.

chinchillas appear. Of course, no one knows if the original gray agouti found in the pet store in 1975 was of the same type as the current mutation.

The coloration of the gray agouti is a pale gray, as its name suggests, with black ticking on the back extending down the sides of the body. In contrast, the hair at the roots is actually a much darker shade of gray. The underside of the body is very light gray, bordering on white, and there should be clear delineation between these areas, as in the normal agouti.

ARGENTE GOLDEN

When this mutation first appeared during 1977, it became known under a variety of names, including cinnamon and golden, although the description of white-bellied golden was probably most apt. It

appeared in a colony of normal agoutis, housed in a North London school.

Their litters contained a number of argente offspring, which could be recognized by the pure golden upperparts, with no dark ticking of any kind. The coloration of their lower parts was again pure white. The tail is golden, and in good exhibition gerbils of this variety, there should be a trace of white hairs running the full length, from the base of the tail to the tip, where they form a clear tuft. The eyes are an attractive shade of ruby red.

Pairings of these argente individuals resulted in similarly colored offspring, so the mutation was established. This has since proved to be something of a milestone in the history of

Facing page: Stuffed toys of this type should never be offered to your pet.

gerbil breeding, because the argente has in turn proved valuable in creating other color varieties. These include the cream, which has resulted from a combination of argente with the pink-eyed white. Also known as the argente cream, gerbils of this variety are a paler version of the argente form.

DOVE

The argente also played a significant role as an outcross for the black. When this mutation was being established in Britain from the imported American stock, breeders noticed that, occasionally, some of the resulting youngsters had a paler coat color. These were the forerunners of the dove-gray colored gerbils which are increasingly popular today.

The gray coloration is of a light shade and should be of even depth. A problem inherited as a result of its black ancestry, however, can be the sporadic appearance of white patches, especially under the chin. Such individuals should be discarded from the breeding program, in order to eliminate this fault as much as possible. As with the argente, the eyes of the dove are also ruby red in color.

In a way similar to the breeding of the argente cream, so the dove has also been crossed with the pink-eyed white to yield a dilute form. This is an even paler shade of gray, often described as the lilac.

OTHER COLORS

The gray agouti has been used in combination with both the dove and argente golden to produce two separate varieties, both of which are known as ivory at present. Another fairly

The agouti gerbil (foreground) has figured prominently in the development of a number of new gerbil colorations, including the argente.

recent development has been the pairing of gray agouti and black gerbils, to yield a so-called blue variety. In reality however, the actual coloration of these gerbils is a dark, blackish shade of gray.

Doubtless, further new mutations and colors will arise in the future. There is a rare chocolate form at the present which is being developed, and possibly before long, mutations affecting the coat itself may

For the beginner hobbyist, the well-known agouti gerbil is a good choice, as it is a very hardy variety.

arise. Already in hamsters, for example, there is a well-established long-haired variety; in mice, satin coats, with a very glossy texture, are relatively common. Such mutations could arise in your first breeding collection of gerbils!

a library or a local breeder for further information. Special show pens for gerbils are used. These not only enable judges to assess the animals with relative ease, but also, the standardized format does not distract from the

A cinnamon white spot gerbil and an ivory gerbil. The latter (the lighter colored of the two) is a new color.

EXHIBITING

If you are interested in exhibiting your stock, then you should join the relevant societies. Ask your pet store,

individual gerbils.

Depending on the size and nature of the show, there will be various classes for gerbils, based largely on their coloration. Try to obtain an entry form and a schedule detailing the classes as early as possible. Write to the show secretary concerned, and enclose a stamped, self-addressed envelope.

Complete the entry form carefully, after studying the schedule of classes, and mail it back in good time before the closing date. Remember to include your entry fees.

Aside from their markings and coloration, the

An albino gerbil and a Mongolian gerbil. Albino gerbils are not frequently seen in the wild, for their coloration makes them subject to predation.

physical appearance (or "type") of the gerbils is important to the judge. The eyes should be large and prominent, while the head itself needs to be relatively broad. Small ears or long noses are two faults in this area which will lead to a gerbil being penalized by the judge.

The tail must be straight, thick, and terminate in a good brush. Deviations, such as kinks, are considered to be serious flaws. The body itself needs to be relatively compact and short. Any sign of a hollow in the back is regarded as a point of weakness in show stock, as is a long body.

Should this seem confusing, the best means of appreciating what constitutes a top quality exhibition gerbil is to visit as many shows as possible, and speak with breeders. You will then build up a clear impression in your mind of what is required, and should be able to judge your stock accordingly.

The poorer-quality animals are best sold just as pets, rather than for breeding purposes, although you do not need top quality exhibition stock to breed winners. But if you are constantly upgrading the quality of your stock, the likelihood of breeding winners on a regular basis will be significantly increased.

Even if you do not win at a show, however, it should always prove a pleasurable experience, because here you will be able to meet and talk with people sharing a common interest. As a newcomer to this aspect of the hobby, you are certain to find a friendly reception in most instances, and advice is usually freely available.

Health Matters

Gerbils, like most rodents, are normally healthy animals, and providing that they are kept in clean surroundings and well-fed, they are unlikely to suffer from disease. But you should always check your gerbils carefully, since recognizing illness at an early stage will improve the likelihood of successful treatment.

A healthy gerbil is, of

Routinely check your gerbil for signs of any abnormalities, such as lumps or bald spots. The earlier a problem is detected, the easier it can be remedied.

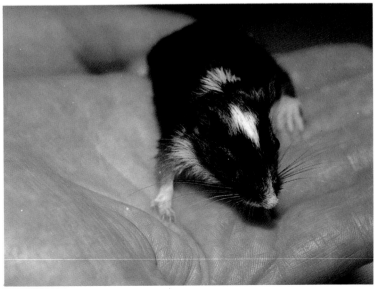

course, bright-eyed and inquisitive, with sleek and shiny fur. Any animal which appears dull and lethargic, loses its appetite, and hunches over needs careful watching, as it is likely to be showing early signs of illness.

If it is part of a colony of gerbils, then you should probably remove it to separate accommodation, in case it is suffering from an infectious illness. Bear in mind, though, that it may be difficult to reintroduce this individual at a later date.

Treatment of gerbils can be difficult, and for proper advice, you should consult a veterinarian, preferably one

A healthy gerbil is alert and interested in its surroundings. The more you observe your pet's behavior, the more able you will be to determine if he is not feeling well.

Gerbils that are healthy are playful and active. If you think your gerbil is ill, a visit to the veterinarian is in order.

who is experienced with small mammals. An injection may be the most effective form of treatment, and this obviously needs to be administered by the veterinarian.

Tablets are rather difficult to give, even assuming the dosage can be scaled down adequately. Medication via drinking water is easy and straightforward, but gerbils do not drink large volumes of fluid. As a result, it will be difficult to ensure that they receive a therapeutic dose.

There is also the further complication that some antibiotics used in veterinary medicine are potentially dangerous for gerbils. These include

Even though gerbils are hardy and can adapt to unfavorable environments, they should not be subjected to sudden, extreme changes in temperature. Additionally, they should not be exposed to drafts.

penicillin, so do not be tempted to purchase remedies from pet stores unless they specifically state that they are safe for small rodents. These may otherwise kill the beneficial bacteria—vital for digestive processes—as well as the harmful bacteria which caused the illness.

TYZZER'S DISEASE

While gerbils are generally resistant to infectious diseases, this particular bacterial infection often leads to heavy mortality if it gains access to a colony. It is more likely to be encountered in a breeding group than in solitary animals.

Unfortunately, there are no clear-cut signs. Affected gerbils are reluctant to move and appear hunched. The fur is dull and held away from the body. Diarrhea is common,

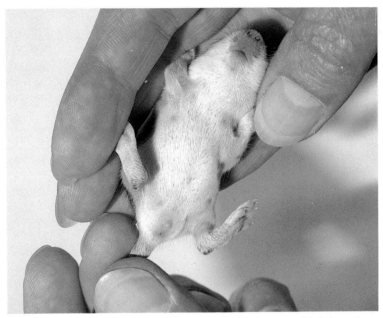

Like other small mammals, gerbils can be stricken by parasitic infestation. Check your gerbil's entire body regularly for any signs of parasites, such as sore and blisters.

especially in young gerbils.

Diagnosis of Tyzzer's Disease can only be made accurately by a post-mortem examination. The causal bacterium, *Bacillus piliformis*, can then be isolated from the liver. In spite of treatment, mortality in a group may well exceed 70 percent. Although Tyzzer's Disease is thankfully rare, you need to be aware of its seriousness and means of spreading.

It can be transmitted from

mice, via contaminated food or bedding, so be certain to purchase these items from reputable pet stores and keep them away from other rodents. This is especially important if your gerbils are housed outdoors, where mice are more likely to gain access to their accommodation.

In addition, always quarantine new gerbils for at least a couple of weeks before allowing them to run with your own established stock. By taking such precautions, you should then be reasonably certain of preventing Tyzzer's Disease from infecting your stud.

DIARRHEA

Although loose droppings may be associated with infectious diseases, they could well be the result of a simple dietary problem. Diarrhea is a symptom, not a clear-cut disease in itself, and so it can be linked to different conditions. It is easy to recognize, since an affected

Gerbils that are housed indoors are less likely to be stricken by infectious diseases than gerbils that live outdoors.

animal will remain huddled—often in a corner—with fecal soiling evident around its anus. The droppings will be loose. This is sometimes also described as "scouring."

Diarrhea may be caused by a sudden dramatic dietary change or by the consumption of stale food. Unsanitary conditions will attract flies to the gerbils' quarters, and this can also lead to diarrhea, as can dirty water. Examine your management, therefore, to try to identify the cause of the problem.

You may decide to leave a pair of gerbils together, even if just one member is suffering with diarrhea, because of the inevitable disruption caused by separating them. A traditional remedy for diarrhea in gerbils is the use of a little powdered arrowroot (available from pharmacists). This can be given on a piece of biscuit, the surface of which has been moistened with water beforehand.

Indeed, it is important to keep up the gerbils' fluid intake, because diarrhea will result in a greater than normal loss of water from the body. As an alternative to arrowroot powder, you may be able to obtain arrowroot biscuits, which are more palatable and equally effective.

Ensure that the cage bedding is kept clean and changed as frequently as necessary. If the anal area appears sore, you can apply a medicament recommended by your veterinarian or pet shop. As always, wash your hands thoroughly after handling a gerbil. This should prevent the spread of infection to other gerbils, or even yourself.

To help prevent your pet's becoming ill, keep his living quarters as clean as possible.

Stick to a simple diet, and if the gerbil's appetite is depressed, it is worthwhile offering dehusked sunflower seeds. You can purchase them in this form from health food stores, or you may simply decide to split off the husks from the seeds yourself. Dehusked sunflower seeds will often tempt the appetite of a sick gerbil.

If you suspect that some other item of food may have caused the diarrhea, then obviously, withdraw this from the diet. In any event, it is probably best to restrict the gerbil to a dry seed diet until it is well on the road to recovery.

Keep the sick gerbil in a warm spot as always, so that it does not need to use its precious body reserves on keeping warm. Recovery should be fairly rapid, but maintain a close watch on the gerbil for several days afterwards, as recurrences can occur.

CONSTIPATION

Sometimes constipation can follow a case of diarrhea, although this is generally a rare occurence. The condition can also be caused by an intestinal blockage. The first obvious sign will be an absence of droppings, and on closer inspection, the gerbil's stomach will appear swollen. Avoid prodding it, since this is likely to be painful.

Start by providing plenty of greenfood, which should have a laxative effect. If no improvement occurs within a few hours, then it is possible that the gerbil could have swallowed something which has resulted in an intestinal blockage. Fibers from unsuitable bedding, such as cottonwool, will have this effect.

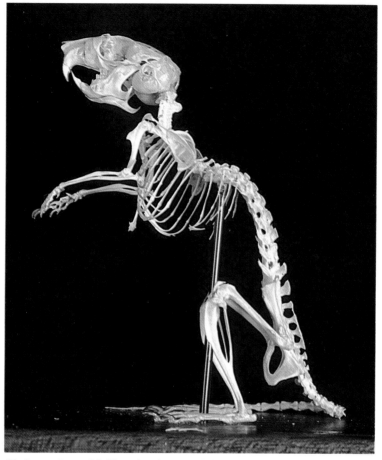

Skeleton of a gerbil. Note the elongated hind feet bones, which enable the animal to balance itself while it squats on its haunches.

This pair of gerbils shows every outward sign of good health.

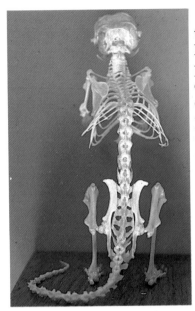

This photo clearly illustrates just how long a gerbil's tail really is. A gerbil's tail is not prehensile: it cannot be used as a means to hold onto something.

As a last resort, it is worth trying either castor oil or liquid paraffin (from a pharmacist). A small drop or two may shift the obstruction, although it is preferable to seek the advice of a veterinarian. In some cases, the fairest option is euthanasia, rather than allowing the gerbil to continue suffering because of the blockage.

CHILLING

This situation is normally encountered with gerbils being kept in damp and drafty conditions, such as a poorly-insulated outhouse or shed. Affected individuals are huddled up, trying to keep warm, and are plagued by runny eyes and nose and a loss of appetite.

Warm, dry conditions and good food will assist recovery. In addition, you must take a careful look at the position of your animal cages. Sheds should always be waterproof and free from drafts. Once animals are properly housed, they are unlikely to contract ailments of this type.

EYE TROUBLES

Unsuitable cage floor litter remains a relatively common cause of eye problems in gerbils. Very fine sawdust or sand, disturbed by the burrowing activities of the animals, may enter one or both eyes, causing irritation, inflammation, and weeping.

Straw or other sharp material may actually scratch and damage the eyeball itself, and this can lead to an infection. Treatment with special opthalmic drops or ointment, applied several times a day, should lead to a speedy recovery. But you must also substitute more

The skeletal configuration of a gerbil's legs enables the animal to jump great distances—considering the size of a gerbil.

suitable bedding, as well as treating the injury itself.

Other similar eye injuries can result from fighting, and if the swelling is pronounced, or certainly if there is any bleeding, then you should seek veterinary assistance without delay.

FITS

Epileptic convulsions are not uncommon in gerbils, being associated with some strains more than others. Affected individuals, especially if they are not used to being handled, may appear to go into a trance-like state, and begin to tremble all over.

If you place the gerbil back in its quarters and leave it alone quietly, it should recover rapidly in minutes without problems. But repeated recurrences are not uncommon, should the gerbil be subjected to any prolonged stress such as

repeated and protracted handling. It may, therefore, be preferable to exclude badly affected individuals from your breeding program if possible.

CANNIBALISM

Another behavioral abnormality, cannibalism is a particular problem associated with young female gerbils producing their first litter. It can result from a nervous temperament coupled with unnecessary disturbance on the part of the owner. There is obviously no treatment, but if it is only the first litter which is cannibalized, there may be no subsequent cause for alarm. However, any female that continues to destroy subsequent litters

Facing page: A nutritious diet is a very important factor in maintaining the overall good health of your pet. If your pet refuses to eat, it could be that he is not feeling well.

should definitely be prevented from breeding again.

Some gerbil keepers believe that this is a character trait which may be inherited. A female gerbil who has repeatedly cannibalized a number of her offspring is likely to produce daughters who in turn also destroy their youngsters.

INJURIES

Bites are the most common form of injury encountered in gerbils, being caused by fighting. Provided that the resulting damage is not too severe, the wound can be treated with a safe antiseptic and should heal quite quickly. Some hair loss may be unavoidable under these circumstances, however, spoiling the gerbil's future show potential.

Injuries to the tail can be more problematical, partly because they bleed very readily. Placing the tail in a solution of potash alum and cold water, made up as directed on the packet, should stimulate the healing process by promoting blood clotting.

Unfortunately, even a slight knock of any kind— for example, the gerbil's mate walking on the injured tail—can damage the frail covering of injured skin, leading to further hemorrhaging. The process will then need to be repeated, although if the blood loss is only from a small area, then a styptic pencil, as sold for minor shaving cuts, can stem it effectively.

Should a gerbil actually break any bones, for

Facing page: Like fanciers of other small mammals, the gerbil hobbyist can increase his knowledge and understanding of his chosen pet through the many fine pet publications available at pet shops.

Above: Your gerbil's bedding should be replaced on a regular basis.
Facing page: This gerbil is obviously well cared for, as evidenced by his beautiful appearance.

example, by awkwardly falling, this can present definite problems. It is very difficult to set a gerbil's tiny bones; thus, the animal's future depends on the nature of the damage.

If the fracture sets naturally in such a way that the gerbil still has a comfortable existence, then it may be kept as a pet, or possibly for breeding purposes, although its exhibition days will be over. A serious fracture may necessitate euthanasia, however, so ask your veterinarian for advice.

On occasion, pet gerbils are caught by cats, and some lucky individuals manage to escape with little or no obvious injury. But you must bear in mind that if your cat damaged the gerbil's skin, there is a possibility that it could have transferred harmful bacteria to the gerbil.

Always consult your veterinarian in this instance, as the use of antibiotics may be recommended in such cases.

In any event, the gerbil will be in a very distressed condition and should be placed back in its cage and left quietly to recover. Do not handle it more than is absolutely necessary at this stage, because otherwise, this additional stress could prove fatal.

BALD PATCHES AND PARASITES

Loss of fur in gerbils can result from various causes. Some of these causes are infectious, whereas others are not, being the result of behavioral abnormalities for example. Some gerbils persistently rub their noses

Facing page: As with handling any other kind of pet that is sick, always wash your hands afterwards.

The skin covering a gerbil's tail is loose, and if the animal is handled in a rough manner, it can easily be damaged.

The gerbil's forepaws are hand-like in their structure. Thus, a gerbil in the wild is extremely adept at excavating deep tunnels—in which he makes his home.

against the cage bars and, as a result, develop a bald patch on their noses. The fur will grow back again within a few weeks if the cause of the irritation is removed. The most effective solution, therefore, is to transfer the gerbil from its cage to an aquarium-type enclosure, where there are no bars.

If the fur loss is caused by disease, then very careful treatment is necessary to prevent the infection from spreading to other members of the colony. Newly-acquired gerbils should always be inspected very carefully for signs of fur loss, because the effects can be quite devastating if a disease like mange is introduced to an established group.

This is a parasitic ailment, caused by tiny mites which live just under the top layer of skin. Youngsters may be infected by their parents soon after birth. As a precaution, therefore, some breeders refuse to breed from an infected animal which has apparently recovered, because of the way that mange is easily spread by direct contact.

The symptoms are relatively clear-cut, starting with small pimple-like eruptions usually present initially on the skin of the hindquarters, feet, or ears. These blisters soon ooze fluid, and then they turn into sores. The fur on and around the infected areas is lost, with the skin itself being dry, flaky, and often inflamed.

When treating any gerbil for mange, the first step should be to isolate the affected animal completely. Its original quarters must be

Facing page: Head study of a gerbil. This animal's fur is in good condition: it is thick and smooth in appearance.

thoroughly disinfected, as should any associated equipment. Obtain a commercial mange preparation, which should be used carefully as directed to kill the parasites. At least two separate applications are likely to be necessary.

If no treatment specifically for small animals is available, then it is best to use one produced for kittens, rather than dogs, as this could otherwise prove too strong. It is also a good idea to supplement the gerbils' diet with pieces of fresh orange or even Vitamin C tablets, as the sick animal may be somewhat deficient in this vitamin.

Treat a gerbil affected with mange only after you have tended to all your healthy stock. This will help to minimize the risk of spreading the ailment to other gerbils. Be sure to wash your hands

thoroughly afterwards.

Gerbils do not commonly suffer from other parasites, although occasionally they may be afflicted with red mites. This is most likely to arise if they are kept in empty bird cages, as in some pet stores, with the mites being left by the previous occupants of the cage.

These tiny parasites are barely visible to the naked eye and often remain concealed in dark nooks and crannies. They emerge after dark, feeding on blood through the gerbils' skins.

Red mites can multiply very rapidly under favorable conditions and are likely to cause anemia and even possibly fatalities among young gerbils before they leave the nest. Treatments such as those used by birdkeepers will probably prove quite satisfactory for use on gerbils and are widely available from pet stores.

Check with the manufacturers if you have any doubt. Repeated treatments will be necessary to kill all the red mites, and the gerbils' quarters must also be washed out properly with a suitable preparation.

Worms and other internal parasites are rarely encountered in gerbils, although they could be contracted from inadequately washed greenfood. The first sign of the problem may be the discovery of an excreted worm in the cage litter, or possibly even a dead gerbil.

It is often worthwhile to have post-mortems carried out on animals that die unexpectedly. The presence of intestinal worms could be discovered as a result, and then appropriate treatment commenced for other gerbils that have been in contact with the deceased animal.

When treating a skin-related ailment such as mange, some hobbyists supplement their pets' diet with vitamin C.

Routine screening of the droppings can also be a useful diagnostic tool to alert the gerbil owner to the occurrence of such parasites in his stock.

TUMORS

Old gerbils may often finally succumb to an internal tumor. Apart from being difficult to diagnose, little can be done for affected animals. If you have any reason to suspect that one of your gerbils is suffering in this way, then consult your veterinarian. Euthanizing the animal will be a likely course of action.

Some typical signs of a tumor are protracted weight loss and a general deterioration in condition.

Below: An albino Mongolian gerbil and her pup. It will take several weeks before the pup's tail becomes fully furred. **Facing page:** Diseases ofttimes related to old age, such as tumors, are not easily diagnosed. Your veterinarian can best advise you on what course of action to take.

Other Species

Having gained experience with the Mongolian gerbil, you may decide to expand your collection to include some of the other species that are now being bred by enthusiasts. Stock can be much harder to obtain, however, depending as on where you live. In addition, many species are actually unknown in collections at present, but more may become available to enthusiasts in the future.

Apart from the difficulties involved in obtaining stock from overseas, however, the animals will almost certainly have to undergo a lengthy period of quarantine when they arrive

A very attractive cinnamon white spot gerbil in a typical gerbil stance.

at their destination. This is likely to prove an expensive undertaking; thus, fellow enthusiasts often cooperate when organizing a project of this type and split the costs.

For further information about official requirements, start by approaching the government department responsible for agricultural matters in your country. Aside from health considerations, you may also need to deal with conservation licensing procedures as well.

All of the following species are already reasonably well established in private collections at the present time.

LIBYAN JIRD

This species is closely related to the Mongolian gerbil, in spite of the

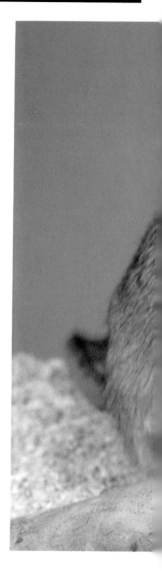

An agouti gerbil. In the agouti pattern, each hair is banded with white, orange, and black.

difference in their common names. Their relationship becomes clear if the Mongolian is referred to under its more zoologically correct name of clawed jird.

In fact, the Libyan jird or giant gerbil, *Meriones libycus*, is very similar in appearance to its smaller relative and resembles the agouti in color. Its body length may be as much as 8 in. (20cm), and the tail is of a similar length, so they need more space.

Libyan jirds tend to be relatively nervous by nature and will benefit from the provision of suitable retreats in their quarters. Otherwise, breeding results will be disappointing. The gestation period is somewhere around four weeks, and about four youngsters are produced in each litter. They should be independent by a month old and need a diet similar to that of the Mongolian gerbil.

A family of Mongolian gerbils exploring their new home. Mongolian gerbils may not be as striking as some other species of gerbil, but they are great pets.

A pallid gerbil industriously excavating a tunnel. Pallid gerbils, which are fairly popular, require the same basic care as that for the Mongolian gerbil.

SHAW'S JIRD

Another member of this genus that is sometimes available is Shaw's jird, *Meriones shawi*. This is similar in size and appearance to its Libyan relative, but has proved more adaptable and friendly by nature.

Pairs can be established without too much difficulty even once they are adult, and they prove generally reliable parents. In addition, especially from a child's viewpoint, they rarely bite, even if they are not used to being regularly handled.

You will probably need to accommodate them in a converted aquarium, with dimensions of at least 36 in. (91cm) long and 18 in. (45cm) wide. Pairs are mature by six months old, but rarely prove as prolific as the Mongolian. Do not allow them to become over-crowded, because tail-biting will then be inevitable.

Fighting is less likely to arise if these larger jirds are kept in pairs, rather than as a colony, unless their surroundings are very spacious. Their lifespan tends to be slightly longer than that of their Mongolian relative, exceeding six years in many cases.

PALLID GERBIL

This particular species became relatively common, at least in Europe, during the 1980s. Pairs have proved keen to reproduce, and so it has been possible to build up stocks quite rapidly.

The pallid gerbil, *Gerbillus perpallidus*, is attractively marked, with pale-orange upperparts. Ticking is confined to the rump, although there is a gray tinge, resulting from the

Facing page: A pallid gerbil with her baby in tow. Very young gerbils are frequently transported in this manner.

coloration at the base of the hairs, elsewhere on the animal. The remainder of the body is white.

Care is virtually identical to that required for the Mongolian gerbil, although pallid gerbils tend not to eat fresh foods with any relish—apart from a little dessert apple. Youngsters are relatively slow to develop following the gestation period, which can be up to 30 days. They should be mature by five months of age and are reasonably easy to pair together even after this stage.

OTHER GERBILS

The Egyptian gerbil, *Gerbillus gerbillus*, used to be seen quite regularly in the

Gerbils are interesting and comical little animals. If you choose a gerbil as a pet, you can look forward to endless hours of enjoyment and amusement.

past, but is now relatively scarce in collections. It is a small species, barely measuring 5 in. (13cm) in size. It is a darker shade of red than the pallid gerbil.

They are extremely social gerbils by nature, and will thrive when kept in a colony system. As many as eight youngsters may be born after a gestation period lasting just over three weeks, and they should be feeding independently by a month old.

Finally, you may encounter the Indian gerbil, *Tatera indica*. This is another large species, with a body size of 17 in. (43cm), and needs to be kept in a way similar to that described for Shaw's jird. They are quite variable in coloration, with their upperparts ranging from a pale shade of brownish-gray through to reddish-brown. The underparts are white.

Avoid unnecessary disturbances during the breeding period, because these gerbils can be prone to cannibalizing their young. It may also be worthwhile, in some breeders' experience, to remove youngsters once they are independent, because they can attack the subsequent litter. This may be a reflection of overcrowding, however, and suitably spacious quarters must be available. Pregnancy lasts up to 30 days, with the young being able to feed entirely on their own after a similar period of time.

Pallid gerbil mother and her pup. This species of gerbil, which does best when kept in a colony, can produce litters which number up to eight in size.

Index

THE PROPER CARE OF GERBILS
TW-106